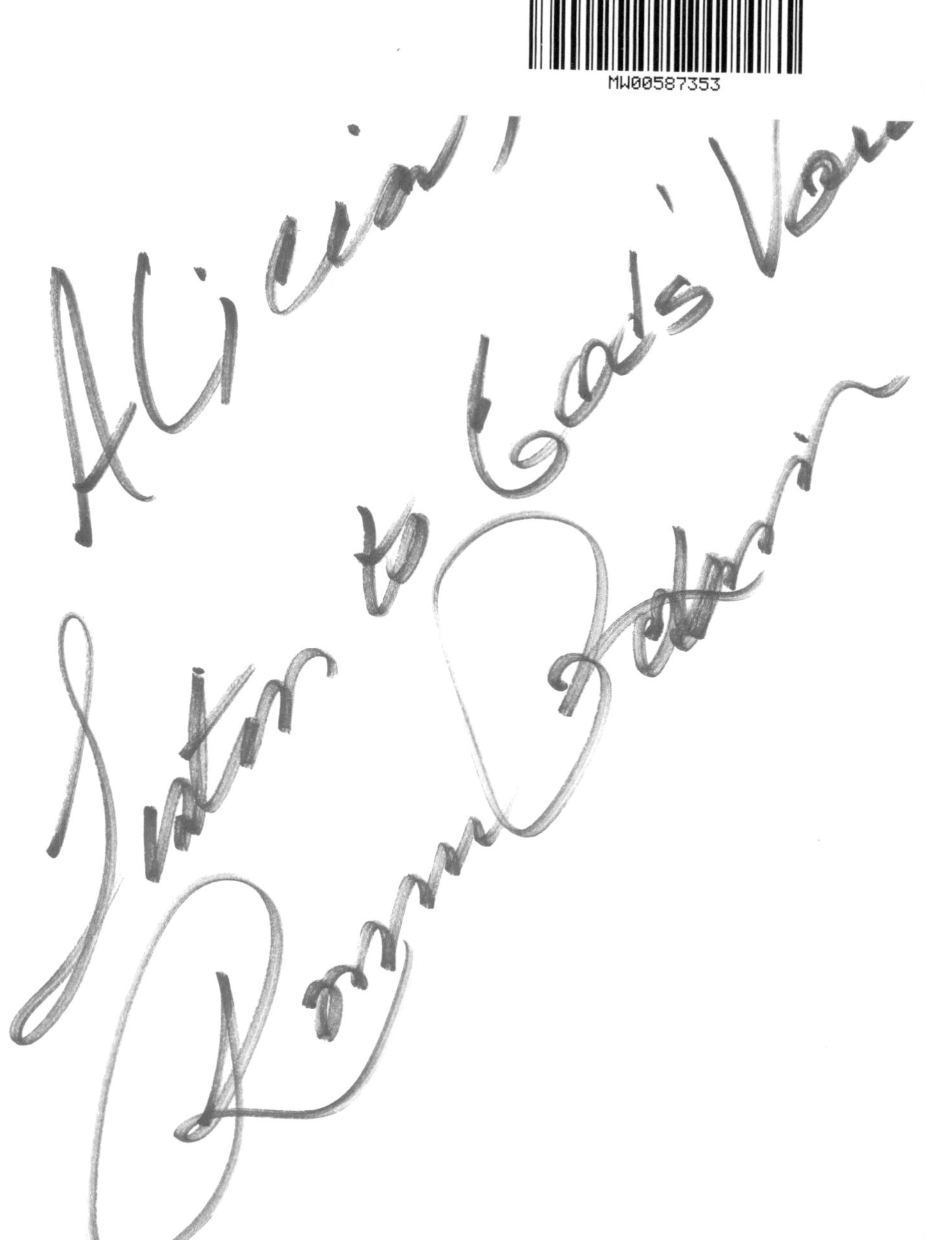
Alicia,
Listen to God's Voice

Your Voice is Your Power

Stop Believing Thoughts Of Fear and Start Becoming Who God Says You Are

Emmy Award-Winning Anchor and Author

Romona Robinson

Contact Romona Robinson:
Website: romonarobinson.com
Telephone: 800-296-8232

Editor: Lisa Bell
Cover Photograph: Eric P Mull

ISBN: 978-1-61244-769-8
Library of Congress Control Number: 2019910258

Printed in the United States of America

Halo Publishing International
1100 NW Loop 410
Suite 700 - 176
San Antonio, Texas 78213
www.halopublishing.com
contact@halopublishing.com

"Listen for God's voice in everything you do, everywhere you go: he's the one who will keep you on track."

(Proverbs 3:6 MSG)

To my late and beloved mother,
yours was the voice that pushed and
assured me that I was good enough
and could fulfill my biggest dreams.

Contents

INTRODUCTION 11

Chapter 1 13
BE AFRAID AND DO IT ANYWAY

Chapter 2 22
STAND IN YOUR TRUTH

Chapter 3 32
FEARING LOSS

Chapter 4 48
YOUR MESS IS YOUR MESSAGE

Chapter 5 62
YOUR VOICE IS YOUR POWER

Chapter 6 74
SLAYING MY GOLIATH

Chapter 7 96
UNMASKING YOUR FEAR

Chapter 8 112
FEARLESS FAITH

Chapter 9 126
NEEDING—AND BEING—A FEARLESS FRIEND

Chapter 10 134
DISCERNING GOD'S VOICE

Chapter 11 147
SILENCING THE ENEMY

Chapter 12 155
HOW HAVE YOU BEEN CALLED TO SERVE?

Chapter 13 169
PRAISING GOD IN THE FACE OF DISAPPOINTMENT

Chapter 14 178
WHEN GOD SAYS, "YES!"

Chapter 15 189
GOD PROMISES AN ABUNDANT LIFE

EPILOGUE 199

ACKNOWLEDGEMENTS 205

ABOUT ROMONA 207

INTRODUCTION

What is your situation? Are you like many women who have been waiting to hear from God about your career, finances, your children, relationships or your health? Have you grown weary, searching for answers as to why God has not come to your rescue? I found the answer to many of these questions, and I hope this book will provide answers for you as well.

Over a thirty-year award-winning journalism career, I interviewed and listened to what keeps women up a night, how they're bombarded with voices of fear, failure and doubt.

This book was born out of those conversations and my own personal stories of living in fear, masking my failures and listening to negative thoughts instead of trusting God.

There were two questions women repeatedly asked me after they read my memoir, *A Dirt Road to Somewhere*—how do you recognize God's voice from your own? And how did you walk through seemingly insurmountable storms in your life?

I believe it's the power to surrender to our thoughts—listening to God. When you allow the outside noise of others to tell you who you are, who you should be and what you'll never be—you've relinquished your power.

Your Voice is Your Power includes impactful, meaningful stories about ignoring society's pressure to measure up—laced with grace, gratitude and sometimes humorous hang-ups about taking back our control by listening to God's masterful voice, which is greater than potentially debilitating voices that can keep you stuck. It's my hope that after reading this book you will do the heart work and head work required and listen to what God says about you, giving you the power to live your best life by using the power of your voice.

Chapter 1

Be Afraid and Do It Anyway

My speech ended, and hundreds of women still filled the ballroom. I laughed and talked to conference-goers as I autographed their books and took photos.

In spite of the many women surrounding me, one woman caught my attention as she tiptoed through the crowd to the front of a long line waiting for autographs. She broke the line, took a deep breath and whispered to the reader about to get her book signed, "Excuse me, Miss, could I please have just a minute with Miss Robinson."

The other woman's eyes narrowed as she leaned over and motioned to the back of the room where the last person in line stood.

But, this young woman would not be denied. "I know, I know. Please excuse me. I don't want a book," she said. "I just need to say something to Miss Robinson."

I turned my attention to her, and jokingly asked, "Oh, so you don't want one of my award-winning books?"

She laughed and replied, "Miss Robinson, I've read it. I got it at the library. That's why I wanted to come here to talk to you. God told me to come here." The words flooded from her. "My name is LaToya. I just need a minute of your time when you get a moment."

As I looked into her troubled eyes, I sensed desperation. Something weighed heavily on her mind. Her demeanor dripped deep pain.

"Of course," I responded. "Just let me finish with my book signing."

"Sure." She planted her small five-foot, two-inch frame into a seat, looking relieved we would talk.

Finally, I finished with the last reader and approached the young woman. "Alright, LaToya. What's up, girl?"

"I read your book, and God told me I should be brave enough to come talk to you," she said.

I nodded. "What's wrong?"

"Chile… I'm wearing a mask. Miss Robinson, I'm a fake, a phony, a fraud!"

Whoa, Whoa, Whoa! What? I stood, utterly floored and puzzled by the words raging from her mouth. She looked tightly put together.

"Why do you say that about yourself?" I asked.

"I'm thirty-eight years old, married with two kids from Mobile, Alabama, and I ain't got nothing to show for it. I have made a total mess of my life, and I'm afraid."

Rodney, my husband, darted a look at me. He knew the conversation could take a while and wanted to make sure I was okay and not ready to leave. I smiled assuring him it was okay. I needed and wanted to take the time to talk to her.

"Why do you feel that way?" I asked again.

"I just feel like I made so many mistakes, dragging my children half-way across the country and back, knowing their dad was not right. I ignored the signs and thought I could make it work. I've been putting on this mask every day, covering up the hurt and fear of my husband leaving the kids and me. I followed him to California and now to Cleveland after he got a promotion, and now two years later, we're separated. To make matters worse, I recently lost my job. I have a college degree, but it's been tough finding work." She paused for a breath. "I'm a Christian, and I love the Lord, but I've been feeling stuck like my life is going nowhere. I wake up afraid and go to bed afraid."

LaToya talked a mile a minute. It was tough to get a word in, but I knew she had so much bottled inside, and she was looking at me for guidance.

"LaToya, I'm flattered you came here to talk. I am going to pray for you and your girls."

I sighed. I have been there. I desperately wanted to reassure her that God had not abandoned her and her daughters. I started with spiritual comfort by sharing two of my favorite scriptures I keep on standby when the road gets tough for me, and I'm faced with uncertain times and debilitating fear, unsure God would rescue me.

Shortly before dawn, Jesus went out to them, walking on the lake.

When the disciples saw him walking on the lake, they were terrified. "It's a ghost," they said and cried out in fear. But Jesus immediately said to them, "Take courage! It is I. Don't be afraid."

"Lord if it's you," Peter replied, "tell me to come to you on the water."

"Come," he said.

Then Peter got down out of the boat, walked on water and came toward Jesus.

But when he saw the wind, he was afraid and beginning to sink, he cried out, "Lord, save me!"

Immediately, Jesus reached out his hand and caught him. "You of little faith," he said, "why did you doubt?" (Matthew 14: 25-31 NIV)

And…

"Now faith is confidence in what we hope for and assurance about what we do not see." (Hebrews 11:1 NIV)

She was quiet for a minute. "Miss Robinson, I love those scriptures and the stories in *A Dirt Road to Somewhere* about faith and how you trusted God during extreme hardship and unfairness in your life. Each time you listened to His voice, things worked out for you. That's why I knew I had to come see you."

"LaToya, remember in the book, I also obeyed God. That's what's tough for us to do. Even if it's hard, if it hurts and if it's scary, listen to his voice and obey him," I said.

"I know Miss Robinson. Please don't forget to pray for me," she said as she stood and turned to walk away.

Rodney, still an earshot away, came over and said, "If you don't mind, can we join hands and pray right here and now?"

"Yes," she shouted as if her life depended on it.

The three of us joined hands in the mostly-empty ballroom as Rodney lead us in prayer.

"Lord Father God, we know where two or more are gathered in your name, there you are in the midst of them, and whatever we ask and believe, we will receive. We know you know all about us and our circumstances. We know you love us. You know all things, God. So Lord, please protect LaToya and her children.

We know your Word says whatever you ask in my name, believe it and you will receive it. So right now, God, we're asking for LaToya to find a job so she can provide for her children. We also know all things work together for good for those who love God and are called according to his purpose.

Thank you for hearing our prayer."

"Amen," we all said together.

LaToya seemed a bit calmer after our prayer. In parting, I encouraged her to trust God and do what He said. "Even when you're afraid, do it anyway."

Ignoring the fear and pushing through the pain can seem impossible when your husband has abandoned you, you have no job, and you're terrified for your children. It can seem impossible even when someone tenderly reminds you to "trust God."

Even after I started to write this book, I had bouts of fear about the message God wanted me to deliver and whether I was on the right course. My confirmation would come days later by way of a little interruption.

LaToya blew into my presence that day like an imminent storm—slow in her approach but quick to deliver her truth. She and I knew God created that moving moment between us.

LaToya emailed me several months later with an update—she had a job, and she and her two girls were happy again. She talked about finally being able to shake loose from the shame of her struggles and blaming herself for the breakup. "I started praising God, being grateful for all the things He's given my girls and me, and things started to change," she wrote.

LaToya was a reminder that God sends what we deem as interruptions and disruptions into our lives for a reason.

That change only happened because she was brave enough to remove the mask, be vulnerable and transparent, and deal with the fear she hid behind. The judgment of family, friends and colleagues can add undue stress, which you easily eliminate when you cast your cares on Him. LaToya realized only God is her judge and jury, and everyone else just has an opinion—opinions that don't pay your bills or move you forward toward God's grace and mercy. She turned to God and let Him fight for her.

I have heard from many LaToya's over the decades who allowed Satan to confuse and convince them of all they cannot and will not be—he feeds on rejection, abandonment and betrayal.

"Romona, I'm struggling to understand why bad things keep happening in my life, and I believe that prayer is so powerful, but he hasn't answered me. When you speak to God, I would be grateful if you remember me."

—Instagram

"I am a strong, educated career woman, yet I'm afraid to stand up for myself. I admire your strength. I've been praying for guidance. How did you find the courage to speak up?"

—Facebook

"My husband just suddenly died. I'm afraid. He was the breadwinner of our family. I've been praying, but nothing's happening. God hasn't answered. Can you pray He will furnish the increase soon?"

—Facebook

"I'm going through sadness this morning, not sure I will ever find love again. I'm beginning to think I deserve to be alone. Your daily posts inspire me."

—Email

"I'm feeling brokenhearted, and I'm moved to reach out to you. I have made so many mistakes. I think God is tired of rescuing me."

—Instagram

"My friend left abruptly and unexpectedly. I was sure I had found my life partner, and I feel so hurt and rejected. I think my prayers have fallen on deaf ears. Maybe God is tired of listening to me. Would you pray for me?"

—Facebook

What I've Learned... Choosing Wrong is a Chance to get it Right

SATAN feeds on people who feel alone and scared in this world.

His is the voice he wants you to hear. He salivates when you make a wrong turn on your journey—when you allow his negative thoughts to infiltrate your mind. He's like a lion waiting until his prey reaches their most vulnerable moment, and then he pounces—confirming all of the bad junk they think about themselves. When you trust God, you can live a courageous and confident life. The confidence comes from knowing that no matter what life throws at you—relationships that end, dreams that die, unexpected illness—God can replant and rebirth a new season. As long as you stick with His Word, He can end the drought of worry. He can bear fruit in your life.

When life's unexpected changes happen, you have the power to create a new vision. Let past failures go and focus on what's in front of you. Even if you have to build a new life, brick-by-brick, there is comfort in knowing God's love and guidance will be there every step of the way.

I believe you have to shift your beliefs and the way you deal with storms in your life.

Stop beating yourself up for choosing wrong. People can hide who they really are for years. And by all means, please be kind to yourself and stop putting everyone else first. When you experience turbulence on a plane, there is a reason you're instructed to put on your oxygen mask first if the plane loses cabin pressure. You instinctively help your child first, but you can't save anyone else unless you save yourself first.

The enemy's voice will tell you all the reasons you aren't good enough, why your partner left you, you're overweight, not attractive and you can't succeed in anything. Those negative voices are like monsters in your head your mind uses to keep you living scared—afraid of making changes and moving forward from a bad situation.

But I am proof God will take your broken and bruised life and use it as a testimony for others. That pain can be turned into an amazing purpose. You just can't go ahead of Him. Put Him in the driver's seat. It's scary. You don't want to wait, but do it anyway—allow Him to block the dead-end roads in your life as you do what He asks. He wants to move you from your troubles to the abundant life He promised.

Chapter 2

STAND IN YOUR TRUTH

As women, why do we hide the truth or flat out lie about what's truly bugging us—our fears, weaknesses, hurts, insecurities and all that keeps us up at night? Where does all the shame that our secrets will be found out come from? I had to find answers to those tough questions in order to bounce back after personal feelings of being broken and incomplete.

I traced the origins of this secretive tendency back to when I was growing up in the late sixties and seventies. Mom and my older sisters marched alongside men and women demanding equal rights and better-paying jobs for blacks. Those years encompassed the time when the feminist movement caught fire. Women spoke up and out about their plight, gender equality, reproductive rights, domestic violence, equal pay, women's suffrage and a myriad of issues.

Yet, I grew up in a home where my mother kept her struggles private. Mom was never shy about speaking her truth inside our four walls. However, she was adamant that we didn't take our personal business out into the streets. She protested daily over how she wanted a better life for her eleven children and how especially her girls needed to ignore the limitations being put on women. At the time, black women wanting a higher education were encouraged to seek teaching or nursing degrees—assuring employment. But mom implored us to go out into the world and use our brains to make something of ourselves in whatever field we chose.

"Y'all are some pretty girls, but you ain't gonna get by on yo looks. Get an education, get a job and be able to take care of yo'self," she ranted.

She raised us not to talk back to her or other grown-ups—a two-edged sword. On the one hand, I grew up with a sense of respect for seniors, but I was reluctant to speak, even if I knew what the elder said was false.

Like many parents, my mom did the best she could, given her challenging upbringing in the thirties and forties. But whether moms knew it or not, they merely recreated their painful past—a past where women were to be seen but not heard, forced to cope with their difficulties and feelings by keeping quiet. Their censure caused fear and pain, creating a belief that speaking up and out in public only caused greater pain.

For many years, the fear I inherited from her compelled me to withhold and question "my voice." It took many years to push past the fear of being judged and allow myself to become comfortable enough to share my stories of heartache, pain and frailty.

I revealed several secrets in my first book, A Dirt Road to Somewhere. One of the most heart wrenching was that I suffered four miscarriages and couldn't bear children. I'd grown tired of hiding the truth of my experiences, refusing to reveal that at times, I felt like less than a woman.

But even as I resolved to tell my story, I could hear my mom in the background saying, "Don't you go out there tellin' all yo business."

I knew, though, for all the wisdom I gained from my mother and the deep abiding love I have for her, she was wrong about this. God wanted me to share because shame thrives in the dark, and we can't fully feel the love of people He's put in our lives if we don't reveal our true selves. Nothing gets healed if you keep it covered up.

I carried a sense of shame and deep despair over something I felt should come naturally—giving birth. The devil's whispers taunted me with accusations that I was barren because my Lord and Savior let my children all die in the womb.

I compared myself to my sisters, girlfriends and colleagues who looked like they were a part of a baby-making factory. Surrounded by little ones, even though overjoyed by each birth, I slowly died inside.

But I knew God had something different in store for me.

Even when writing my memoir, it was still difficult to completely swallow the truth serum and tell the whole truth about everything going on inside me. I can now because I feel the pull of God, showing me it's okay to be completely transparent as I walk in my truth. I feared I'd be labeled as a dry, old hag. At forty-two, I married Rodney, and we spent tens of thousands on IVF treatments to get pregnant.

Like so many women, when life's problems came to my door, I suffered in silence. Afraid to lift the veil on my pain, I dreaded potential judgment. Worse, I didn't want friends and family to pity me.

My sister urged me to share her substance addiction struggles in my book. However, I worried about being so transparent. I didn't want her to be scrutinized, shamed or blamed for what transpired between her and her child, which I agreed to care for and raise when she could not.

I didn't want anyone or my family to know about the fiancé who left me laying on a cold floor, bleeding after surgery while he was out cheating with another woman—I feared the stigma of being weak in their eyes.

I was afraid, but God's voice kept beckoning me, assuring me He was with me. Something amazing happened when readers shared with me how those raw, authentic, vulnerable stories forced them to take off their blinders and start to deal with the emotional drama in their own lives. Many said they would never write a book about it, but they were willing at least to take an inward look and discover why they felt the need to cover-up their pain. It helped many to know that a woman of prominence could relate to their everyday struggles and heartache, knowing she, too, made mistakes.

God taught me through the process that there is grace and mercy for missteps. God allows us to make mistakes, so they become our testimony. And He invites us to share with others so we can learn and grow together. Our voices connect us and make us stronger when we follow God's voice.

To get real, we have to walk away from fear, risk failure, and stand boldly in our faith, no matter how faint it feels. We have to believe God is strong and loves us—and we have to act accordingly.

"Rise up; this matter is in your hands. We will support you, so take courage and do it." (Ezra 10:4 NIV)

Even when we lean on God's Word, in public, our human body still wants to put on new skin and hide the layers of hurt we feel.

But know there is healing in your transparency and truth.

When we pull back hidden layers and speak our truth, only then do I believe we start allowing God to move us into our purpose.

Our vulnerability makes us most human, most beautiful, most like each other. But we choose to hide behind a mask, afraid of unveiling the truth about our imperfect life. I get it—I've done it and lived it too.

When I truly gained insight into my behavior, I was able to understand the reason behind my fear better.

Looking back, what if I shared with my girlfriends and family how I suffered inside, feeling old and barren and like an incomplete woman because I couldn't perform a natural function God created in all women—a vessel to procreate? How might that tormenting time have been different? Now, I know they would have nurtured me, providing the love and comfort I needed to get me through such a traumatic time in my life.

While growing up, Sister Johnson at my church was so open and transparent about her troubles. She was not afraid to stand up and shout before us all. I wish, even back then, that I understood why.

Every Sunday, I'd hear Miss Johnson during the pastor's sermon. "Yes, yes, yes! Lawd, Help me, Lawd. I need you. Thangs have been so tough on me, Lawd! Every thang's goin' wrong, Hallelujah! You so good to me, Lawd Jesus! I praise yo name, Lawd!"

Miss Johnson—one of the elders in the church, was a white-haired, seventy-year-old, heavy-set woman with a pleasant face and warmhearted smile. She usually wore bright floral dresses to church, even during the winter. Sweat formed around her temples the more worked up she got, praising God, jumping up and down in place, wide-eyed and screaming at the top of her lungs. The old folks called it "gettin' happy" when she was moved by the Word of God being preached by the pastor.

Her loud outcry drowned out the pastor, the choir and any musical accompaniment—usually the organ or piano. The louder her shrieks, the more my sisters and I let out belly laughs, covering our mouths so as not to be heard by the grown-ups who looked back and scowled at us for the disruption.

The adult parishioners used to whisper about what might be wrong in Miss Johnson's life. Did her man leave her? Was she broke or sick? But Miss Johnson stood unashamed before God and all of us.

Mom always believed when you allowed yourself to be vulnerable or flaunt your weaknesses that people might attempt to take advantage of your troubles. I learned over the years, some of Mom's teachings were spot on—being open and truthful with some people should come with a caution sign. Spilling your heart to the wrong person about your failing marriage, poor health or financial woes can carry risks. Devious people could use the information against you for ill-gotten gains.

But fear of sharing your heartache forces you to hold a mirror up to your life and ask yourself some tough questions. The key to healing is to deal with the problem or pain—even if you decide to keep it private, with God's help, deal with it.

Step one for me was to stop blaming myself. For years, I tortured myself for not conceiving children. In my mind, twisted thoughts of the many mistakes I made raged.

"If only I had not put my career first and married sooner. If only I had done things differently, maybe harvesting, freezing and storing my eggs when I was a lot younger, they would have been more viable, giving my babies a fighting chance. Or maybe if I were not so frazzled in a highly stressful career."

A lot of "I should of, would of, could of" taunted me. I needed to silence those voices, from myself, from others, from Satan. They were not God's voice—the only voice I wanted to guide my life.

In my quiet moments of solitude, I can still harken back and feel the agony and pain I endured, questioning any bad decisions I might have made to cause infertility. Sometimes, you just have to be your best friend and talk to yourself, encourage and remind yourself, you are not your past failures.

If it didn't happen for you, it wasn't meant for you, and God has something better in store for you.

I found amazing comfort in Psalm 147:3 (NIV), which says, "He heals the brokenhearted and binds up their wounds."

The Lord was my strength in dark times. When I fell into deep despair over being childless, he got me on my feet again. I was on a turbulent, emotional road to nowhere—misery attached itself to my brain.

But God charted a new course for me—one that involved children, just not my own. One that invited me to take new, scary steps like sharing my voice.

I found incredible strength in His Word only when I stopped lying to myself, pretending to be okay, and when I admitted covering up my pain and asked Him to help me. He often uses our brokenness and confusion to recreate a beautiful purpose.

"Through the praise of children and infants you have established a stronghold against your enemies, to silence the foe and the avenger." (Psalm 8:2 NIV)

The cure for my heartbreak came by way of a child. She would drown out the enemy talk. The email came from an 11-year-old girl shortly after my last miscarriage. I left one television station and explored the idea of leaving Cleveland. She feared I might leave town, so she implored me not to abandon her and the thousands of Romona's Kids I worked with for over thirty years. Romona's Kids is an Emmy-nominated television program, turned institution I started in Cleveland 30 years ago. It empowers and encourages our youth to find their specific path. Her email read like the wisdom of someone decades older.

She wrote, "Miss. Robinson, I know you just left your television job. I hope this doesn't mean you're leaving Cleveland.

I want you to know how much your words of encouragement and being present over the years has meant to me. You are so important to us kids. We need you."

What I've Learned... Shame Thrives in the Dark

Life has a way of taking us down some dark, lonely roads of despair.

We can be hard on ourselves—believing we're unworthy, don't deserve happiness, we created the pain in our lives so we should just sit in it—some question what they even have to offer God. The schemes of the enemy distort the truth to fit the pain you're going through.

I've had a lot of bad breaks. I've been fired, I faced a health crisis, I've been in a dark place, a place of desperation and despair following miscarriages that threatened to take me out. I've been duped, dogged and disillusioned. I dealt with fake friends and blind loyalty. I lived in fear for so many years, afraid of telling my truth, but my faith in God kept telling me it was time to step out of my comfort zone and share what I learned.

You're probably a lot like I was—still battling new conflicts I fight even today. But countless women confided in me that when they removed the mask, stopped listening to outside voices and started believing what God says about them, they truly began to heal. Don't sit in your suffering but thank God for moving that painful situation or bad people out of your life.

Through it all, God taught me He will mend the hurt, but only if I first admit I have a problem and deal with it.

When I faced my vulnerability and insecurities, stopped lying to myself that I'm okay and putting on a fake face for the outside world but then suffering in silence, He was there.

God will be there for every step, bringing other people to walk alongside us on scary paths, waiting for us to discover our truth, share it with others, and follow His way even in the face of fear. Once I began speaking my truth, I watched God work wonders in my life. Keep reading and discover how.

Chapter 3

FEARING LOSS

Most of the dozen or so cabbage seedlings Mom and I planted in the chill of a March Missouri morning did not produce the bountiful thick, green leafy heads she hoped for. Three months later, the first signs of summer appeared in our country garden, but the cabbage leaves wilted and curled, bearing a discolored bright, yellowish-green hue. Visible holes, revealing specks of sunlight, shined through a leaf or two.

The anticipation of a plentiful June harvest always danced through my mind, waiting for Momma to work her magic in the kitchen and preparing homegrown vegetables—what we called rabbit food—into something special, fully deserving of savoring each bite.

When I was five or six years old, I got my first "on the job" training in gardening. I call it a job because Mom was very particular, measured and skilled when it came to her prized possession. Through discipline, care and confidence, she could grow just about anything she set her mind to. She learned a few cost-saving tricks by talking to folks at our local general store. But mostly, as a young girl, she watched her daddy hand plow his forty acres of land with nothing but a mule. He died when she was twelve years old, but he left her with long-lasting lessons of hard work and the value of seeing a project through to the end.

She also knew being successful in the garden was critical since she was raising 11 kids on a shoestring budget as a seamstress.

Born out of necessity, her love of gardening became her passion. She found comfort and joy and seemed to cast her poverty-stricken, single-mom cares aside.

I worked in Mom's garden on and off for the better part of 25 years. I would throw on an old t-shirt and worn shorts and sprint out to assist Mom with whatever she needed. I could dig holes, carry twenty-pound containers and buckets of water from the outdoor faucet next to the front steps. I hauled buckets of animal feces from our chicken coop to use as fertilizer. But my favorite time was when she allowed me to sow the seeds. No gloves needed as mom encouraged me to become one with nature, to drop down, bend over on both knees and help her plant dozens of vegetable seeds. I loved the feel of fresh-tilled soil in my tiny hands, poking holes and helping Mom plop in the seeds, and then smothering them with the sunbaked soil.

Even today, if I close my eyes, I can smell the fresh produce that sprouted from the earth and feel the warm wind in my bangs. I can hear how mom spoke to her plants—barking at those that hadn't kept pace with the expected maturity timetable, praising others that exceeded her growth expectations. She gently stroked the leaves carefully—nurturing them as if they were one of her newborns.

On warm, muggy days, big bees buzzed over our heads, chomping at the bit to continue pollinating plants and surrounding wildflowers near the garden. Pesky mosquitoes hatched, hovering, looking to feast on our moist bodies, and they did most days. I still itch just thinking about Mom swatting with the towel thrown over her shoulder, trying to fight off the bloodsuckers. At times, she slapped me on the jaw or smacked me on the forehead to kill one that landed on my face—a moment that always drew a belly laugh from the two of us. We could never afford any of the costly repellants folks talked about.

But that particular year, caterpillars set up shop, feeding indiscriminately on a variety of plants. What should have been a dozen scrumptious looking cabbages—green compact balls with distinctive leaves formed in a dense rosette—instead, looked like something poked, plucked at, and chewed on.

As she stooped over, Mom's back arched. She extended her arms to inspect her row of lifeless, droopy cabbage. An exhausted moan escaped her mouth from a long day of backbreaking, finger-numbing work as a seamstress on the assembly line followed by this disappointment.

"They worthless, no good," Mom said. "Cabbages are easy growers. I've done this time and time again."

"What killed them, Momma?" I asked.

Mom is slow to speak, puzzled by the loss. "Maybe they got too much rain. It could be they got too much sun, or it was too warm this sprang. I reckon it probably was worms. I see signs of cabbage worms."

I cringed. The first time I encountered a dead worm, I jerked back and screamed. It was greenish in color, one or two inches long, glued to a dead cabbage leaf. Its spongy skin resisted my pull when Mom instructed me to remove it.

"Momma, there's another and another," I screamed.

"Romona, it's okay, they all dead," she said, reassuring me. "Just pick 'em off the leaves. They can't harm you."

"I'm afraid, Momma. They are nasty looking."

"Things die. It's just God's way."

Mom used our solemn scenery in the garden to plant scriptures in me. The worms and the wilted cabbage were both times for her to explain that we all return to dust, but our spirit returns to God in heaven, who gave us life. As a child, I found the words tough to comprehend.

"All humanity would perish together and mankind would return to the dust." (Job 34:15 NIV)

I struggled to understand why. Why did the cabbage die? My mom worked hard, and we needed the food. But as I grew, God showed me He could make meaning from loss, even the biggest losses, and He was with me, even when I didn't understand why I had to go through so much pain.

* * * *

On January 31, 2018, shortly before 8:00 p.m., I received a phone call from another younger sister, Melissa. I put her on speakerphone, knowing she called from my mom's hospital room at University of Missouri Hospital in Columbia, Missouri.

"Romona, Mom's in trouble," she blurted.

"What kind of trouble?" I asked, desperately.

"She can't breathe." Melissa's calm firmness unnerved me. "They're working on her."

"Who's working on her?"

No answer. A faint murmuring from a group of unknown voices came across the speaker. Sound bounced around, creating well-like muffling. I pictured a group of doctors working in a tight space. A thrusting noise caught my attention as I strained to make out the whispers of one, maybe two or three people. A violent lunging or pushing, coupled with short, frantic orders drove me to my feet.

"What's happening, Melissa?" I demanded.

"The doctors… Mom can't breathe. It's bad, Romona. She's not responding." My sister's voice choked with emotion.

I shouted. "No, Melissa. She's coming back." *Mom is tough. She bounced back from three strokes. She'll beat this one too.*

I caressed my ears, shutting out the noises. "Breathe, Momma. Breathe. Please!" I paced back and forth, convincing myself she could hear through my sister's phone. I begged God to breathe life back into her.

The clock flipped to 8:22—more than 20 minutes.

"What's going on, Melissa?" I kept repeating. A flood of images plunged through my mind. A man's voice ripped through the speakerphone as someone approached Melissa and my other sister, Rena, who waited for his words.

"We did everything we could. She just stopped breathing, and we couldn't save her." His somber voice offered little comfort.

The words produced an avalanche of grief like a swirling tornado, touching down with blunt-force winds so fierce they knocked me onto my bathroom tile floor. I can't recall if my hands and knees helped break my fall, but I felt no physical pain. But my heart crumbled under the agony. Heat encapsulated my head. I screamed out to God, "Please bring her back."

Rodney's large frame was no match for my exploding grief. He tried to comfort me, but I pushed him away with supernatural strength. Another wave of heat jolted my head, and this time, blood gushed from both my nostrils. An internal fire raged through my body.

Rodney suggested calling an ambulance.

"Don't you dare!" I needed no medical attention. I wanted no paramedics, no doctors. I only wanted my momma.

"How could she just leave me," I screamed. I tore away from my husband running to our bed, maybe because it's the place I felt safest. I buried my head in a pillow, hoping the soft cottony cushions would somehow ease my excruciating facial pain.

"I was just with her two days ago," I screamed to Rodney.

Sinking back into that memory helped me calm down into my grief. When I'd seen her two days before, Mom was extremely weak after having a mini-stroke and a full-blown seizure. She bounced back as she had after her first, second and third strokes over the previous six years. This time was different, though. She was much weaker, slept a lot more and mumbled a lot.

Dementia started to set up shop in her brain, robbing her of precious memories of her life and children. For three days, I walked softly in her hospital room, hoping she would not be overwhelmed with nine or ten of her kids and grandkids visiting at the same time. Each day, hooked up to a host of hospital monitors, IV's and feeding tubes, she stared at me, never uttering my name. Her glossed-over eyes and straight face told a harsh tale.

She had no idea who I was.

That knowledge burned an emotional hole in my heart, even though I understood the disease shows no mercy to anyone.

On the fourth day, her demeanor and appearance stunned me. My sister, Evonne, finally managed to get a comb through her beautiful thick, white hair, which had endured several days' worth of surgical tape supporting neurological monitors and wires, which they removed. The feeding tubes also gone, she wanted to eat food, and her eyes, no longer dull and lifeless sparkled bright with joy.

"Romona, Romona, you're here," she cried out as I moved to her bedside to hold her hand. "When did you get here?"

I wanted to cuddle next to her, tucked in like a child when we watched our favorite TV shows together.

"Yes, Momma, I'm here." I ignored her question. "How are you feeling?" Purposely shifting to a soft tone, I squeezed close to her on the edge of the bed, stroking her hair and face.

"When did you get here?" she asked again.

"I've been here four days, Momma."

"You have?" She rubbed her forehead three or four times with a dazed look, searching her thoughts.

"It's okay, Momma. I know you knew I was here."

She smiled, staring straight at me as if she could see through to my soul. "Romona, where am I goin' when I leave here?"

"What do you mean, Momma? You're gonna get well and go home where you live with your daughter, Rena."

She stroked her head again as if she had a tension headache, puzzled, trying to comprehend my response. "But where am I goin'?"

I glanced up at Melissa, perched on the other side of Mom's bed, hoping for a suggested answer. Melissa shrugged her shoulders.

"Romona, where am I goin' when I leave here," she insisted. "Is it a pretty place? A house? How does it look? Describe it to me. How many bedrooms?" A smile grew across her face as she waited for my response.

"Yes, Momma, it's a beautiful house. It's spacious and has bedrooms and is pristine—I know how much you love a clean house." I poured love into each word.

I clung to my last precious memory of Mom, smiling at me, pleased she was going somewhere beautiful after her hospital stay.

As I remembered that moment on the day she died, a scripture she taught me came to mind.

My Father's house has many rooms; if it were not so, would I have told you that I am going there to prepare a place for you? And if I go and prepare a place for you, I will come back and take you to be with me that you also may be where I am. You know the way to the place where I am going." (John 14:2-4 NIV)

I knew God has a room for all of us who believe in Him and receive Him, but I was torn and caught off guard by Mom's persistence about where she was going. I wasn't sure if she was asking me to describe heaven as her final resting place. Even though, in the back of my mind, I knew what she was asking. Fearing her loss, I wouldn't allow myself to believe the end was near. I prayed God was going to provide another miracle as He did several times before after a stroke. I also knew dementia played tricks on her mind, so maybe, by chance, she forgot what my sister's house looked like although she had been staying there.

Her questions haunted me for several months. I wanted a do-over. A chance to tell her I knew exactly where she was going. I wish I eloquently described God's house, her final destination. I know she's living in a majestic home, one filled with beauty and joy, not the pain and sorrow she suffered in the end. I hope it has the most beautiful garden, packed with her favorites. I pray it glistens with sparkling emeralds, topaz and opals—her favorite stones. I hope it's adorned with beds of roses and multicolored lilies—her preferred flowers.

"Out of body, present with the Lord." The Bible says that when we pass, we're immediately with the Lord. Free from pain and suffering, our bodies are restored to health. (2 Corinthians 5:8)

Even with the knowledge of exactly where Mom now resides, the pain of her loss crippled me. I wanted someone or something to make the pain go away. The grief was overwhelming. Fear and anxiety took hold of my mind, body and spirit, wracked with endless emotions. Deep sadness penetrated me, questioning whether I did enough, said enough before she left. Some days, my body felt frozen, preventing me from moving past the pain. It was as if I stood in the middle of the street during rush hour. I knew oncoming traffic could crush me, but my body suspended in numbness, incapable of stepping to get out of the way. I wanted and needed to talk to my momma.

I tried to comfort myself by remembering her and the lessons she taught me.

"Yea, though I walk through the valley of the shadow of death, I will fear no evil; for You are with me; Your rod and Your staff, they comfort me." Psalm 23:4 NKJV

This scripture always made me feel safe and secure in God's arms. But, I found little sustainable comfort in prayer, family, friends' or strangers' words—they were only temporary fixes. I hungered for something other than time to feed my empty soul. I struggled to get out of bed, but I had to. Before mom's passing, I had been on a book tour promoting my memoir. I dedicated it to Mom, and I thanked God she got the chance to read it months before He took her.

As a television journalist and author, I had work and book commitments. I forced myself to live up to my contractual obligations.

I cried many times in front of total strangers at speaking engagements as I talked about Mom's strength, hard work, and determination to provide for her eleven children. She did that with little help from my dad, refusing to go on welfare. My mom was so proud of her children. She beamed with pride after I realized my dream of becoming a journalist. She loved hearing the stories of the famous people and presidents I met and interviewed. Most of her calls months before she died were to talk about politics and to get my take on what was happening in the country.

Just like when I was six years old, watching the CBS evening news with Walter Cronkite, Mom and I were still news junkies.

Suddenly, I wanted to quit the job I endured so much to achieve. I didn't want to write anymore—even though I recently declared before Mom's death that my second book would be the next chapter of a storied journalism career. I was absolutely miserable and content staying that way.

Where had my faith in God gone? Where were the unshakeable faith and no fear I professed in my first book that encouraged readers to hold on to God's promise? I knew John 3:16, where the Bible says Heaven is given to all who believe in Jesus. But the heart wants what it wants, and I wanted Momma back.

I saturated myself with scripture, listening to God's voice, begging him to take the pain away. I cried a river of tears every day. I screamed out, wailing, often asking God why He took her. Why didn't the doctors prepare us? Why did I ignore all the cues from Mom that she was tired and wanted to go home—practically begging me to describe her final resting place, a place free from all of her worry and pain? Eighty-three years is a good long life for anyone, but I was not ready. I listened to her voice on phone messages she left me a week before she died. I kept playing them on speaker over and over again.

"No More Tears" eye drops became my best friend—only a temporary cure for daily bloodshot eyes formed from a marathon of misery. I lied to my doctor when she asked how I was coping after the loss—asking if I was sleeping and eating right. I knew that look in her eyes. She was ready to prescribe medication or convince me to see a grief counselor. I told her I was managing well without mom. I was not going to take anything or see anyone I thought would numb the memory of my beloved mom.

I once read the greatest tribute to the dead is not grief, but gratitude. Over time, I began to live that way.

Five months after Mom died, I got a text message from Rena that God used to help me move forward in my grief. Rena is a master at the art of country gardening through her razor-sharp memory of Mom's teachings, sprinkled with her own curious, zesty personality. She remembers all of Mom's advice and instructions down to a science. Things like the planting zones for southeast Missouri, when to sow, how to plant, the perfect blend of soil and natural fertilizer, how much water is needed, if the plants love full sun or shade, when to use seedlings instead of seeds, the tricks and shortcuts to producing a great harvest. Rena's garden rivals Mom's. I once flew into Columbia just to harvest sweet potatoes with her and smuggled some back to Cleveland in my suitcase. Yes, homegrown sweet potatoes, if done right, are just that good!

Her message included pictures of her garden that summer. The pictures attached to her text sent a wave of emotion straight to my head like the swiftly flowing waters of the Mississippi River I grew up fishing in with Mom. The photos of her beautiful collards and turnips, lettuce and cabbage reminded me of the bountiful harvest

Mom used to produce. One photo of Rena nourished my heart with joy. About five-feet-eight, she hovered over her sweet potatoes with the fluorescent sunlight gleaming off her glossy, black hair and chocolate, moist skin with a satisfying smile that signaled her garden success.

Looking at the pictures immediately beckoned me back to the late sixties during some of my first childhood lessons in the garden with Mom—back in that row of cabbage lost to worms. That day, Mom told me not to worry. All things die—just throw the worms back in the dirt and cover them up. They turn to dust. It's just God's way.

The long-ago day became a biblically teachable moment, preparing me for loss. As a child baptized at six years old and having accepted Jesus Christ as my Lord and Savior, Mom knew the importance of all her children knowing the Word. She understood we would all suffer loss someday—even life without her.

God used Rena's colorful garden creations to snap me out of my trance of pain and into the idea for writing this book. The photos lit a literary fire under me—a fire I tried to dim. It felt like God wrapped my chilled, frightened heart in one of the warmest, coziest blankets you could imagine. Suddenly, I could think back with gratitude, a multitude of lessons learned in Henrietta's Garden. The nourishing and healing power of organic food started racing through my mind. Each fruit and vegetable Mom grew had a story to tell and a connection—a parallel to real-life issues and problems we all deal with.

It brought me from my self-pity back into awe of Mom's God-given tenacity. Mom didn't wear many masks in life. She tried to hide her heartache and pain from struggling to raise her children as a single mom. However, she met the challenge of her responsibility, working one and two jobs so my siblings and I might succeed. She endured an early life of broken dreams and plans busted by hardships, abandonment and pain. But later, the strong and courageous woman who taught my siblings and me so much wisdom went back to school, got her GED at 68 years old, and entered college at 70, majoring in computer science! Wow. That was my mom.

During my emotional storm of sorrow and loss, I stayed focused on the fear of living without her and didn't leave room for all of her triumphs over adversity nor our intimate memories in the garden and the lessons God taught her that she imparted to me. She and I shared some of the greatest joys and biggest challenges there. She left her children with the gift of gardening—an art form not to be rushed.

I had forgotten Mom's teaching about her relationship with God's creation of the seeds, good food that could and would sustain us if times got hard. But it was time to remember. It was time to write. Henrietta's garden went from something I hadn't thought about for decades to a treasure trove of thoughts I could no longer ignore. The memories spawned joy again. God used the recollections of nurturing and spiritual adventures in the garden patch with Mom to heal my body naturally. My heart is still a work in progress. But now when I think of the loss of Mom, fear that I can't live without her doesn't enter my mind. I smile mostly knowing she left me with a skill that not only can fuel my body but feeds my soul as well.

What I've Learned...
Healing After Loss

If you've suffered a loss, I hope this chapter gives you the strength and comfort to grab those special memories of your loved ones who have gone on to their final resting place.

Nothing can bring back a loved one, and the pain is so real. But choosing to be grateful is a gift from God, and it opens the door to new life even after the toughest loss. Only God can bring beauty from our pain, but He creates splendor in abundance when we open our hearts and let go of our fear.

This scripture was shared with me as I tried to heal and move on without Mom. It brought tremendous comfort in reminding me God was right there.

"The Lord is close to the brokenhearted and saves those who are crushed in spirit." (Psalm 34:18 NIV)

God will use your pain to help others whose hearts are crushed. Speaking at a trade show after mom's passing, a 20-year-old approached my table, curious and seeking a book that could provide her healing.

"What's wrong?" I asked. "You look so unhappy?"

"I recently lost my dad," she replied. "He was my everything. I suffer from chronic anxiety, and it's been crippling. He's all I had. I feel so alone, and I cry daily."

"You're not alone, are you? You have other family?"

"Yes, my aunt." Tears welled up in her eyes. "And I'm seeing a grief counselor."

I stood to embrace and hug her tightly, sharing my recent loss, and there was an immediate connection, a bond over grief. As she walked away, there was an instant soothing of my aching heart.

Suddenly, I was thanking God for five decades with my mom. She only had two with her dad. When we're in the midst of our pain and sorrow, it's easy to forget others have endured loss at a much younger age and coping and adjusting to a new normal can be devastating. God always has a way of showing us there are people in far more pain than we are. Even during our grief, they need comforting words and support.

I pray you find peace in the indelible marks your loved one left on your life—precious thoughts that can't be stolen, stored memories that can never be deleted, and tender, treasured moments between just the two of you.

Chapter 4

YOUR MESS IS YOUR MESSAGE

I lay on my side in a fetal position, forcing my face into a pillow on my bed. My silk-blend light gray duvet cover and matching sheets were a crumpled hot mess while I rocked back and forth, sobbing. My hands wandered between my head and stomach forcibly rubbing them, searching for a comfortable position to ease the intense pain. I ran my hands through my brown wavy hair. My mascara, eyeliner—a full face of makeup—smeared onto my linens. Excruciating cramps wrenched as if someone reached into my stomach, rearranging things. I wailed in agony and forced my legs closer to my chin.

"Romona, what's happening? What's wrong?" Brian, the man I had been dating, hovered over me, fretting beside my bed. A tall drink of mocha latte with piercing brown eyes and a body that rivaled the ROCK, his body indented the edge of the mattress as he sat next to me. He searched my face as I continued to wipe away tears.

"What can I do? Should I call a doctor, 911?" He reached over, rubbing my shoulder, trying to provide comfort.

"No, no, my doctor isn't in on Saturdays," I shouted.

"Then, what do I do? What is happening to you?"

"Brian, it's my birth control pills. I need them so badly. Most women take them to avoid pregnancy, but my doctor prescribes them also for my lack of estrogen. Without them, my body goes into shock, producing excruciating cramps, and soon I will break out in hives all over my face and body."

"What? Oh, my goodness. I had no idea." He paced around the room.

But it was all a lie, an act—an Oscar-worthy performance by me, I might add. I wasn't sick at all. No pain. Fake tears. It was all a test to determine the truth.

It all started the day prior.

Brian and I had been dating for four or five months. He stayed for the night, and I woke up to perform my daily 9:00 a.m. ritual. I reached over to my nightstand to grab a few multi-vitamins, and my birth control pills—only this Saturday morning, my contraceptives were nowhere to be found.

A creature of habit, I keep everything in one spot so there's no guesswork. I know where everything is. My clothes, my work make-up is separate from the personal stuff, important papers in a file cabinet, shoes, towels—you name it. I know where I put everything. My friends tease that I have a mind like a steel trap.

So how could my pills go missing? They seemed to disappear in thin air.

"You're ovulating," he said in a panic, scouring the room for my pills.

"What? How do you know I'm ovulating?" I shot back.

"I just meant, if you were..." He recovered, speaking softly as if he wished he could swallow the comment.

A surreal thought filled my conscious mind. *Oh, my goodness. I'm ovulating, so missing two tablets in a row could definitely produce an unplanned pregnancy.*

I was in trouble. I couldn't reach my doctor until Monday. I frantically turned my bedroom upside down searching for those little pink pills—my lifeline. I pushed the nightstand forward away from the wall and bed. I flipped it over on its side. Desperate, I flung everything out of its two drawers—magazines, pens, paper, jewelry. I almost dropped my 40-inch television as I yelled for Brian to help me move it off its stand. My mind told me they couldn't be there, but my hysteria would leave no piece of furniture unturned.

I yanked all of my bedding onto the floor, shaking linens wildly, hoping my pills surfaced. It took seconds to dismantle my three-tiered dresser drawers—slinging all of their contents onto the carpeted floor.

I tore from the bedroom, ripping through every inch of my home like a crazed woman. I stuck my hands between the crevice in every sofa or chair—even the guest bedrooms I hardly visited. We moved potted plants, raised rugs—anything that wasn't tethered was a target. Every nook and cranny searched. One or two hours later, Brian suggested we give up.

I took a deep breath and assessed the situation. I was a 38-year-old Christian who vowed not to have children out of wedlock. It's a promise I made to myself as a teenager after watching my mom struggle to raise my siblings and me alone. I also held a high-powered position as a Cleveland television anchor. I lived in my dream home, a role model and enveloped by the love of family and friends. Life couldn't get much better—but if I got pregnant before I was married, I feared I would lose it all.

Brian had been talking about marriage since we first met, asking a lot of questions about the kind of man I wanted to marry, if it mattered that he had an office job, if I had a timetable for marriage, did I want children, what I would do if I got pregnant. At the time, I thought he sure asked a lot of personal questions for only knowing me a short time, but I blew it off.

But that morning, in my bedroom with my birth control pills missing, it all started to make sense. He knew I was ovulating! I didn't even know my ovulation schedule.

All the sudden, I recalled my answers to his probing questions. "I would never have children out-of-wedlock—my mom implored us to wait to get married because she had it so hard raising us as a single mom, and besides, with my job as a public figure and role model, that would not be kosher. If I ever accidentally got pregnant, I would have to get married or probably lose my job."

Thinking back, Brian was so inquisitive about my life, thoughts, concerns, habits—a lot of *what would you do if...?* They were questions I answered freely and honestly, not knowing he was filing the answers away until the opportunity to trap me presented itself.

I began to think maybe I hadn't misplaced my pills. I knew they couldn't just disappear. I knew me. I was a nut for neatness and order when it came to the important stuff. Was Brian really plotting to get me pregnant and force me into a quickie marriage?

Someone took them, and that someone had to be Brian. But how could I prove it? So, I hatched a plan to fake an illness—one so severe he could not stand by and watch me suffer.

After a while of moaning in my bed, I rolled my body out and told him, "I need to go to the kitchen for some water." I brushed off his offer to get it for me while I rested. I wanted to give him enough time to make my pills reappear. He took the bait.

Upon my return, he shouted with a look of relief, "Romona, look your pills are right here. They were stuck underneath the nightstand. How could we miss them after all that searching?" The sincere puppy-dog look seemed convincing, but I knew better.

There was no way I missed the pills. I flipped that nightstand onto its side, and my eyes did not deceive me. There were no pills.

That was the day God opened my eyes. Looking back, I saw signs of deceit from the start. I chose not to listen to the voices alarming me of a problem. I dismissed them.

My earliest clue came on our first date when he told me he had been divorced for two years. I later found out he had been separated for only four months. Confronted, he chalked it up to him being so nervous about our date and enamored with my company that he must have accidentally said two years. He also said he had a six-year-old. My visits to the apartment he shared with his friend and roommate were few, but the absence of pictures of his child should have lent pause and been red flags. After ending our relationship, I found out he had a nine-month-old infant.

Why was I so ready to excuse his lies? If I'm completely honest with you and myself, I had been longing for a serious relationship. I had a burning desire to find a man I could build a life with, so I ignored the facts staring me straight in my face. I also lacked strong, unwavering faith that if I waited, God would send the right man.

Brian had an answer for everything, and that particular day was no different.

"I must have mistakenly knocked them off your nightstand. The thin pack must have slid underneath the nightstand when I pushed it searching for them. I just don't know how either of us didn't see them."

But surely, he could see by my face that his words weren't working.

"Girl, I just love you and want you for myself," he stammered. That was probably the closest thing to a confession he was capable of mustering up.

I choked back the language I wanted to use and simply said two words. "Please leave."

As he walked out the door, I felt so foolish. All of the signs were there. It all seemed so obvious after God opened my eyes. Deceit can be a tricky thing when perpetrated by someone intimately close to you. But that day, I made a CHOICE to flip the script and seek the truth through deception. I made a choice to accept the gift God gave me—clear eyes—and walk in faith from that day forward.

Some of us rationalize irrational behavior. We accept it because the alternative seems too tough to deal with.

Like so many women, I refused to accept the obvious, until I saw the cost I was paying was too much, and the alternative I feared was really the path to freedom.

Even early in our relationship, Brian showed me many signs he was not right for me. He asked countless questions about where my girlfriend and I were going. He yelled at a group of men at a Cleveland Browns game who screamed out in harmony that they loved me. The incident almost came to blows when he took exception to their friendly and harmless cries of affection. Or, during a station Christmas party, a couple of my male colleagues gave me a friendly and tasteful embrace to say hello. He seethed, saying he didn't want another man to touch me—ever!

That should have been a stop sign. But I shrugged off those warnings, making excuses for him. "Oh, he's just protective of me. He's not used to my celebrity."

Truthfully, I could feel his controlling nature. At first, it felt somewhat flattering, but it was a warning sign I chose to ignore. Over time, I became comfortable with the discomfort, and I overlooked the overwhelming evidence of trouble. Like many people, I was innately trusting, but I realized I needed to recondition my mind. I should have been able to follow my intuition and trust myself, along with my feelings. That voice in my head recounted all the evidence of a toxic relationship, but my desire for the relationship to work overcame my God-given internal voice of truth.

When I started to pull back the layers of my life and relationship, I could finally see the real Brian—a deceitful person I allowed to take up space in my life, a man who attempted to change the direction or block my path. I wanted what I wanted, and I also feared and cared about the perception of others. *Romona, a pretty girl who couldn't keep a man, a woman who put career above all else and is a failure at love.* At 38, I looked around, and all of my girlfriends either were married or had kids. I had a great career, but I felt the emptiness and absence of a real connection with someone I could build a life with. I wanted it, felt I needed it and craved it at great cost to myself.

If I had been able to put aside my wants and needs and stare truth in the face, I could clearly see a relationship on a road to nowhere. But God opened my eyes and barricaded that road. Any residual feelings I had for Brian ended that day. I knew my heart needed time to catch up. But my decision was final.

I knew God was not pleased with my sinful and devious behavior. I know the Bible says, "Vengeance is mine says the Lord I will repay," but when you focus on earthly things and find yourself in the midst of betrayal and treachery, waiting upon the Lord can be tough. Our raw, human emotions kick in, and we try to take down our enemy in our own strength.

I realized that day, this wasn't a battle with Brian—it wasn't a battle with me. It wasn't even a battle with selfish desires. It was a spiritual battle—not one against flesh and blood but against spiritual forces. Demons don't fight fair, though. They will use every weapon at their disposal to get what they want, sometimes wrapping them in pretty or handsome packages that go undetected and infiltrate your life committing their evil deeds. It's important to guard your heart against unscrupulous people. But it's also vital to realize we can't win spiritual battles without God's help. I learned that God would link you up with angels here on earth and give you the grace and supportive people you need to fight any problem or evil.

God gives us the tools we need if we continue to follow his Word.

God is with us, but that doesn't mean it's easy. It's tough waiting on God in a society where there's so much pressure to have this and that, to be married at a certain age, to have a degree, to have an impressive job. We become frustrated when God refuses to work in our timing, and we wonder if he really loves us.

At other times, we want to sit and wait for Him to do it all, and nothing changes. We call it faith, but faith requires action. God is working in our lives, but he's waiting for the change within us.

While God's grace opened my eyes that day, what happened afterward required me to think, to act, to change.

I started to question why I kept meeting duds—men who were not right for me. All of my relationships fell apart.

Two years prior, a suave, well-known, debonair businessman in town swept me off my feet, taking me on trips across the country, wining and dining me at fine restaurants, Broadway plays and shopping trips. I later found out he was near broke and charged it all to his credit card. It was supposed to be an initial investment he was banking on to pay huge dividends when he married me.

A mutual acquaintance contacted me to reveal the scheme, saying he felt bad because he knew I was a good person and didn't deserve the evil plot that man perpetrated against me. I saw him as one of those angels here on earth God put in my path for protection.

In the months after I told Brian to leave, I sought quiet, prayerful moments of solitude when I could truly be honest with myself and with God. I realized the common denominator in all of my failed relationships was myself.

It was tough to look inward and avoid blaming other people. What role did I play in the mess in my life? Was I the problem? Could I be choosing the wrong guys? What changes did I need to make?

I had become so good at playing the blame game, bashing every failed affair. But when I truly took off the blinders and got a good glimpse at the truth of my life, I admitted I was choosing all wrong. I was in charge of the choices I made. I was going for the same type of man—extremely attractive, articulate and who appeared to have it going on. Even though I was never into the must-haves like corporate titles, fancy cars, and pedigree, loving the Lord was a requirement. But time and time again, I found being a God-loving Christian was a mask men wore. They lured me in with stories of finding Jesus and being a Bible-carrying, church-going Christian.

I also knew it was finally time for me to grow from reading God's Word to believing in His power, knowing without a doubt if I allowed Him to direct my path, I would meet my forever mate. I had to increase my faith in His promises.

So, I decided to put an end to any relationship going nowhere. God put up roadblocks to force me to see it, but I tried to go around His plans for me and create a narrative that fit my idea of a perfect relationship. I vowed I would not waste my precious temple, the woman God created me to be, in another useless relationship that was dead on arrival, just to fit in and have someone on my arm.

As a matter of fact, I made a pledge to my then one-year-old puppy, Velvet. I brought home the two phonies, and she could sniff them out with her doggy radar. That pint-sized poodle barked non-stop at both of them as soon as I made the introduction.

"Velvet, meet Brian." She growled. "Velvet, be a nice girl. He's a good guy." Her growl got deeper, the longer she scowled at him.

"Dogs usually love me," he said, rolling his eyes.

"She's just protective of her mommy," I said as I put her in her kennel, avoiding making him uncomfortable.

So I told Velvet, no more of these men. I told her I would change.

Despite Brian's tricks, I came out unscathed, but so many other women who stay with controlling men face real dangers, some with deadly consequences.

While I had to heal from the hurt I experienced, I was glad to have the chance to learn and grow stronger from my disappointments.

My personal journey revealed a truth about me I ignored. I was a good person, a trusting soul to a fault at times, qualities for which I will never apologize. But it was time to learn and grow as a woman.

Many wonderful men could love me and treat me well, but first, I had to love myself enough to know I could be alone and still be okay. I made a pledge and promise to myself after those break-ups not to have an intimate relationship again until I met the man God would truly send for me. I waited a little more than two years before I met my husband. Waiting didn't mean, I sat on the couch though. I had some of the best times of my life, working, volunteering, traveling, and supporting women and children's groups.

I no longer feared what others thought of the single anchor, nearing forty with no man and no prospects. There is no shame in admitting we live with a multitude of fears in our lives. It becomes a major part of our testimony. Every person struggles with some kind of fear, and when we face it head-on, we can begin to deal with it. When I stopped worrying about being "found out" or judged, I could truly "see me." I could take a deeper, more spiritual look at who I am and what I wanted in life and for my life. When I was brave enough to say, "I will not accept being taken advantage of, mistreated," then I began to gain strength.

If you're feeling stuck in the same patterns, afraid you'll never have the life you want, give voice to the problems you face. Speak it. Yell at it, and deal with it head-on. Instead of saying the other person has to be changed, or needs to be fixed, reclaim your power. Don't waste your pain. Don't keep repeating the same mistakes. Let go and learn the lesson from it. God will help you when you follow Him.

Many women try to be what we think a man wants, but it is enough simply to be who you are. I had to pivot away from the problem of wanting a partner and wait on God, trust him, believe Him, and ask Him to prepare me for a husband.

I'm not proud of my tactics of getting to the truth. I am flawed, and we all fall short. At times, I freely and willingly sinned when it suited my purpose. I know now God will use our troubled lives to turn our mess into a message. I now protect myself not by being guarded but remembering God sees all. He is the redeemer. God blocked me from those toxic relationships. He had something better for me. I just had to learn not to run ahead of Him and let Him lead.

What I've Learned...
Abuse

Only you can change the direction of your life and head to where God wants you to be. It doesn't matter if you've been traveling down the wrong road and went around His barriers and hooked up with the same characters. There is still time to turn around.

When faced with getting out of destructive relationships, your mind might be overloaded with dizzying thoughts that make your head spin—telling you all the reasons you should stay. (At least I have a man. He may not be my soulmate, but I'll settle, he shoves me a little but only when I upset him.) When we want something badly, our mind will create excuses. That's why it's important to know whose voice is speaking the truth and which is poisoning your thoughts with lies.

I've never been in a physically abusive relationship, but I've gleaned critical information from victims and abusers through countless stories I did on the subject as a journalist. I learned from abusers themselves that they prey on and seek out a specific type of woman. They already marked you and knew your traits and habits—what you will and won't tolerate and how you will react. The first time he shoved you or emotionally and verbally abused you while dating was a red flag. But we make excuses. "I upset him—it's my fault." I gave you two personal examples in my life with dating an extremely controlling and devious man.

Some relationships drain you and suck all of your emotional energy as long as you allow it... and then they go back to committing the same offenses, and you accept living in the same space of emotional bondage.

Some survivors of abuse told me they felt they were to blame and were ashamed for allowing it to begin, and by the time they wanted out, they felt trapped. Others told stories of watching their mothers being abused, and it was all they ever knew. For others, it was low self-esteem, searching for love even if it hurt.

It's never too late to forgive yourself for putting up with a toxic relationship—move on, learn and continue to grow. You can give of yourself without allowing yourself to be used and abused. You can love a person and not allow your heart to be abused by them.

You have to take personal responsibility for your growth. Growth is not automatic. Trust your journey and don't become naive.

You can move past picking the same type. Looking back, I dated famous and financially successful men, not because I really wanted to. It was fun. I knew within a week or two they weren't marriage material, but I was having fun, and that was okay as long as I didn't end up marrying them. I knew a cheating dater would become a cheating husband. It never entered my mind that I could change him if I married him.

If you find yourself in a place you don't want to be—a place where you're not safe, not valued—decide to get out, to find God's path for you, and seek the help you need to get away and move on. There is support available, and you are worth it. Don't give up until you are living the life God has for you.

Chapter 5
YOUR VOICE IS YOUR POWER

In the fall of 1983, I died.

They told me the news director made the announcement in the newsroom. A colleague who was on his way to work saw a serious single-car crash involving a Channel 13 news vehicle along the side of a scarcely traveled two-lane back road. The reporter saw a Missouri trooper looking down at a black female on a stretcher, covering her body with a white sheet. Since I was the only female of color at the time, he assumed it was me, and the sheet was always a tale-tell sign the victim expired. He described the mangled news car, with busted windows and a caved-in roof, to my news director. At a quick glance, it would be hard to believe anyone could walk away from that crash, let alone survive it. So he rushed to tell the station I died in a car crash on a country road in Missouri, and he watched them place my body in an ambulance.

It all started on a misty, cool and foggy morning right outside Jefferson City, Missouri. The wet air gave way to a chilly breeze, and the large oaks and maples had lost their red and gold leaves. Hundreds of giant evergreens flanked the tiny road. I can hardly recall all of the details, but I remember a chill in the air because I wore a jacket, which they later cut off me in the hospital emergency room.

I headed to nearby Columbia, Missouri, with another reporter-photographer in the news vehicle to cover a raging fire. My partner, who was driving, had bouts of road rage, yelling at cars going the speed limit, but he indicated they were not driving fast enough, impeding our rush to get to our assignment. The speed limit was 50 or 55 miles an hour, but I could see the speedometer. He was driving 65, at times pushing 70.

For the umpteenth time, he approached the boiling point toying with whether to pass on the slick country road, which was a short cut to our destination.

I protested loudly. "You know, that's a little fast for this wet road. There are a few levies."

"My speed isn't the problem," he shot back. "It's why you keep turning me down for a date. That's what I want to talk about."

"For the tenth time, I don't date people I work with. I just don't think it's wise." The tension of his driving had me on edge for this repeated, uncomfortable conversation. Maybe that was his plan.

"Is that the real reason or is it just me?"

He was a tall, slender man, about 6 feet and somewhat attractive and about fifteen years my senior. At the time, I thought he'd be a nice catch for someone older, but as a youngster in my first television job, I was not interested in an older man and especially not one I worked with. For months, he repeatedly pestered me on the job for a date.

I should have known from the first hello there would be trouble—the way his eyes canvassed my entire body, traveling aimlessly from one part to the other. It was my first sign that he was like an old, skilled lion that knows how to track its young prey, concealing his intention. He waited for an ambush when the unsuspecting target was caught off guard. Each day I felt like a young buck as he quietly and carefully clocked my movement, anxiously waiting for the right opportunity to make his move.

To fit in and not make waves, I ignored his long stares and wandering eyes. I thought it best to avoid his advances. Looking back, I wish I'd had the courage to complain and tell management how uncomfortable he made me feel. Honestly, I feared retaliation from him or possibly losing my job if I went to management about his intimidating, verbal harassment, which had become an almost daily occurrence.

But that day on the road, I found myself in a cramped space with my aggressive suitor. I couldn't turn around like I did countless times in the newsroom hallway to avoid the predator when I saw him. I sat a few inches from him, buckled up and strapped in a car pummeled by his words laced with bitterness and envy.

"Do you think I'm too old for you? Is that it?" he pestered. "I'm not as young and attractive as you. Maybe you think cos you're pretty you can be picky."

"Please don't take it personally. I don't feel comfortable dating a colleague," I responded, trying to stay calm.

"Why not? Is that really it or am I not your type?" By this time, his volume rose to shouting.

"It's not you. I've just decided I don't want to mix business with pleasure."

Suddenly, the surroundings took my mind off our chilly conversation.

Another car was backing out of a driveway onto the road, visible to us only after we jumped a levy at high speed. He faced a split-second decision—either slam into the vehicle or swerve violently toward a utility pole to avoid it. He chose the latter. While my partner laid on the brakes on the slippery highway, trying to avoid our head-on meeting with a utility pole, my entire body stiffened as I braced for sudden impact. I opened and shut my eyes for a few milliseconds. Thoughts swarmed my mind about our certain death.

"Oh, God. Oh, God." I remember the final word I screamed. "Momma!"

The car swayed left to right. Our heads bobbed up and down, the seatbelts tightened. I distinctly recall the force of the crash as the car cut through what sounded like high weeds, rocks or other debris—a sign we had left the paved road. The car lifted and twisted in the air before landing in a ditch. If not for the ditch to slow the vehicle, the trooper said we might have hit the telephone pole head-on.

Dazed and feeling broken and bruised, but very much alive, I must have lost consciousness for a few seconds. When my eyes opened, my partner was right up in my face, caressing my arm, screaming into my ear, asking if I was okay, if I was hurt.

I murmured, "I think so." But pain covered all of me.

He immediately started to apologize, saying he was sorry for arguing with me, asking me please to forgive him for the crash and injuring me. I wondered, even then, if he was trying to redeem himself, or buttering me up before troopers arrived and peppered us with questions.

He tried to give me a crash-course in how the accident happened (pun intended). He wanted us to be on the same page—that it was not his fault.

"You saw that the car was backing out onto the highway, right, Romona? Do you remember? I screamed, 'Hold on, Romona. I'm going to have to go off the road. Romona, you do remember, right?" he persisted. "My only mistake was not reacting quickly enough, and maybe I swerved too much to avoid that car. Isn't that what you saw, Romona?"

I said very little, more concerned about whether I had any broken bones. A cruiser's flashing blue lights blinked continuously. Then I heard what sounded like an electric saw directly outside my door. Still strapped in my seatbelt, my mind was foggy, and my body hurt all over, especially my neck. Someone yelled my name.

"Romona! Romona! We're going to get you out of there. Stay still and calm. We're going to have you out soon," they shouted.

A flurry of activity buzzed outside our car. As I tried to lift my body up to peer out of my window, I saw a couple of troopers, sheriff deputies, firefighters and an ambulance on the usually isolated rural road. In the distance, someone directing traffic yelled for onlookers to move along. I tried to see if my news partner was okay, but from what I could see through my peripheral vision, he was no longer in the driver's seat. Extreme pain exploded when I attempted to move my neck to my left. My seat was jammed about two-and-a-half feet from the mangled dashboard. The shattered windshield contained a hole the size of a golf ball. My indented door looked inoperable. With no airbags, despite calls for me not to move, I scooted forward a little from my seat to find that the dash trapped my legs underneath, and I couldn't move them. Realization hit me hard. I wasn't merely strapped in my seatbelt—I was trapped.

The drilling outside my door got louder. As I slowly looked to the right, I saw a young male EMT and another rescuer using the "jaws of life," a hydraulic emergency tool used to assist in the extrication of victims in a crash. It cut the door off completely, exposing my entire body, still trapped. The glove compartment, so close in proximity, felt like it was resting on my chest. They used a tool to push the mangled dashboard slowly forward, away from my body, toward its original placement. As the lengthy process of removing me from the car progressed, they hit me with a battery of questions.

"What hurts?"

"My head and neck," I murmured.

"It looks like your head hit the windshield, creating that hole. Thank goodness, you were wearing a seatbelt. You've got a visible bump forming already. Don't worry. We're gonna get you out of here and to the hospital. Just stay as still as possible. Please don't twist your neck. How many fingers am I holding up? Can you feel your arms and legs?"

My news partner came into view in front of the vehicle, peering in at me while pacing back and forth, animated, as a trooper appeared to be questioning him about what happened. He motioned toward the roadway—I assumed explaining why he had to avoid the vehicle. I wondered if he shared how fast he was going.

The EMT barked orders at me again as he noticed me trying to lift my head and body up to peer out the window to see the pole we'd just missed by landing in the ditch.

"Romona, we need you to stay completely still. We're not sure what injuries you've suffered," he explained. "You and your partner are lucky to be alive. Thank goodness, the two of you were wearing your seatbelts—God was at the wheel."

He had no idea how untrue that statement was. It was a madman at the controls. God decided it was not our time.

They slowly and carefully extracted me from the vehicle. I heard the stretcher wheels rolling across concrete and then grass. Three, or maybe four, men lifted me onto the stretcher. I think even my colleague was helping or maybe just watching—my mind was still foggy.

The State Trooper leaned over me. "Romona, can you tell me what happened?"

"I honestly can't remember right now."

Drops of water hit my lips and teeth as I spoke. It had started to sprinkle scattered showers again. The specks of water falling on my face increased.

The trooper said, "Don't be alarmed, but I'm going to cover your face with the sheet, so you don't get wet."

It must have been at that moment when my colleague from the station drove by, witnessed the kind gesture, and assumed I had expired.

Later, after my neck and the bump on my head healed, I returned to work. Called into my News Director's office immediately, he wanted details and said not to leave out one bit of what happened.

He told me the troopers said the news vehicle was traveling at a very high rate of speed. He wanted to know if that was true. I made the mistake of not reporting the repeated harassment before, but I would not this time. I told him the truth—that my partner and I had been arguing about me refusing to date him, and he became upset and was driving way too fast on the rain-slicked road.

Not long afterward, that reporter was gone.

As I tell my story from decades ago, I'm thankful for the way God protected me so many years ago, and I'm grateful for the #MeToo movement today. This powerful and effective movement against sexual harassment and sexual assault has put American businesses and predators in seats of power on notice. No longer should women be subjected to unwanted advances and widespread prevalence of assault and harassment in the workplace. Most of us have been living in it long before social activist Tarana Burke, began using the phrase "Me Too" and it was popularized as a 2017 hashtag.

Like so many working women, I was afraid back then but should've told my boss anyway. I wish I had been brave enough to plug into my power and trust God to protect and provide for me—but thoughts of losing my job kept me quiet.

As a friend reminded me, "Romona, your perceived power… We had none back then. We were so happy to crack the glass ceiling as female journalists we just accepted some of the crap that came along with it."

Now, the ugly little secret—that broke God's heart all along—is a roaring voice that's screaming, "No more," for women everywhere. I'm not foolish enough to believe all harassment will end with #MeToo, but the veil has been lifted and "Times Up." I am stronger today—and would not tolerate that behavior.

I want to encourage women to see their value in God's eyes, feel empowered and take action immediately. Your Voice is your Power. Our silence allows sexual harassment to breed without being exposed. Report the bad behavior, stopping the behavior in its tracks. Keep a calendar with dates and times and what was said. Know your company's discrimination and sexual harassment policy. As a new employee, we usually toss those employment manuals aside to collect dust, but there is critical information in those pages about your rights if you find yourself in trouble at work. Know your rights. Educate yourself, so you know what to do if you are retaliated against for filing a complaint and where to turn for help. Make sure there is a paper trail of your complaints. That way, managers can't claim they were never informed of a problem.

No matter whether your harasser is on the job, in the church, at your school, or wherever, there is no one best way to handle things because every situation is different. It is, however, crucial that you make sure your harasser knows his or her conduct is unwelcome. Be brave and tell that person his behavior offends you and makes you uncomfortable.

Even today, problems aren't always addressed properly. I've received several emails and calls from women and girls who reported incidents, and their employers and schools were slow to take action, so they quit or dropped the accusations fearing repercussions from management and the harasser the company coddled and protected.

No matter how your report is handled, make sure you confide in supportive friends, family members, and other colleagues about the abuse. Taking action is difficult, and you'll need the support of people who care about you and can show you God loves you no matter what. You might find out some of them have suffered the same abuse from your perpetrator. Not only will telling others about the harassment provide support, but it can also be important evidence later.

I did not confide in anyone—not my mom, sisters or even my boyfriend at the time. I feared they would tell me to go to management, and then my older and more talented colleague would deny my claims, and I'd get fired.

As I look back, I realized God saw my desperate situation. He loved me and rescued me, even by means of a scary car wreck.

What I've Learned...
Plug into Your Power

God wants you to step out of your comforts, protect yourself and do the work needed to heal your mind, body or soul. He wants us to walk by faith, not by sight because things we see can be deceiving. It's important to lead with our senses at times and not our heart. He wants us to use the power in our voice to make changes in the world—fight injustices, serve others, stand up for truth and so much more. I was so afraid of speaking my truth as a younger woman. I didn't trust that God would always be there to rescue me, so I put up with a lot and became bitter in the process.

I remember breaking up with a guy, and he called me every name under the sun.

"You Stupid B, you stupid B," he yelled. "You won't find another good guy like me."

He wailed as I opened my front door without uttering a word to allow his exit. He quickly turned back and made a gesture with his fist, as if he were about to hit me. I flinched, and he laughed.

I would see him around town for years, and every time, my body tensed while anger came into my heart. I carried around that hate and hurt, and it grew into bitterness. I knew it wasn't good for me, and I had to remember what the Bible says about forgiveness. So, I decided to forgive him. The forgiveness was not for him, but for me. I had to release all of that stored-up rage.

Disappointments of the heart can trigger countless emotions from anger, pain and bitterness. Stop thinking about the mistakes and failures you've had in the past and keep trying. There are so many lessons we learn from our mishaps.

When you stop running from your hurts and stop suppressing your truth, you will start to see God's favor in your life and where he wants to take you.

I now measure the power of my voice not by what I say in front of people, but what I whisper to myself when I'm alone.

I had to reclaim my power. I am full—full with being me, standing in and living my own truth. I haven't always been brave or courageous, but life's bumps and bruises have a way of forcing you to find that inner strength. It was important that I listen to that quiet, still, inner voice, which was God whispering words of encouragement and strength.

You, too, can get the transformation you crave. With a potent concoction of self-confidence, determination and taking action, you'll discover you have the passion and power to do the work God put you on this planet to do.

Chapter 6

SLAYING MY GOLIATH

I was a newlywed in 2004, preparing for my honeymoon and filled with a mountain of anxiety. I was keeping something from my new husband, Rodney—I was deathly afraid of water and especially the ocean.

He knew I couldn't swim and was somewhat fearful of the water, but he had no idea the depths of my fear. It was a heart-pounding, soul-stirring formidable giant. In its presence, I felt so small, like David facing Goliath. With God's help, David had done the unthinkable—overcoming his foe—but right then, my fear was winning. I knew this was the time to stand up to it—to conquer it, or fall prey to it forever.

Rodney heard me tell stories of crazy escapades my girlfriends and I experienced as young, vibrant singles when we traveled extensively. I had been on expensive party yachts docked or near the port. I had visited too many beaches along the Atlantic and Pacific to name. But I didn't let on that my irrational fear of the ocean wasn't just your run of the mill phobia like hating spiders or snakes or fearing heights or cramped spaces. No, my fear was bigger than that—much bigger.

It grew to this colossal size when I nearly drowned. At 22 years old, living in my first apartment in Jefferson City, Missouri, I enjoyed my first job in television news and every luxurious amenity I could afford. I lived in a two-bedroom, spacious apartment with a gorgeous private complex pool. Raised in rural Missouri, it was the first time I could remember seeing or certainly having access to an in-ground pool. Even though I never learned to swim, I loved going out, dipping my toes in the soothing, summer water or wading in the three-to-five foot deep section. The unsupervised pool had an emergency rope and big, bold markings on the inside of the pool to let swimmers know where the deep end started. I didn't dare go near the drop-off to the seven-to-nine-foot end.

On one hot afternoon, I decided to use a giant, bright-yellow rubber-ducky floating device I retrieved from the complex's equipment room to kick my legs in the shallow water and get some exercise. The duck stretched four to six feet in size. There were three or four teenagers also at one end of the giant pool—maybe two boys and a girl. The enormous pool was about 40-feet wide by 70- or 80-feet long.

I periodically dipped my head underwater as I flung my arms over the floating device, holding on tightly as I kicked my legs, trying to keep them above water—practicing my swim technique and form. I was a huge fan of swimmers in the Summer Olympics, and I loved the precision with which they raced from one end of the pool with seeming ease—though I knew the skill, practice and dedication to their craft. I told myself I would take swim lessons as soon as I got some real time off from my new and demanding job. That day never seemed to come. As a rookie, I sometimes worked seven days a week, at times fourteen hours a day. But for the moment, I splashed about, laughing and having fun with my own company. I felt so relaxed and carefree.

Suddenly, the rubber ducky hit the concrete side of the pool, and I lost my grip. No big deal—it had happened many times before. I would stand up in the shallow water and go fetch it. Only this time, I could not stand up. My feet were not touching the bottom of the pool. Instead, my head sank a little underneath the water, my eyes shocked by what I saw in a flash. The blue and aqua sun-kissed water was above my head. My eyes opened wide and shot across the pool to the bold black and blue font on the interior of the structure. "Deep Water," it read. "7-9 Feet."

"Oh my God," I thought, filling with fear. I had ventured into the danger zone of the pool—at least for non-swimmers—without knowing it. I had been kicking underwater with my eyes shut on Mr. Ducky. I didn't notice how dangerously close I had gotten to the deep end.

I panicked, frantically kicking, flapping my arms and hands, and trying to scream. I went under slightly, my head mostly covered with water, and I felt my hair floating above me. My head bobbed above water just enough for me to breathe. In shock, I didn't know what to do. I tried screaming again as the icky chlorinated water entered my mouth. I had a burning sensation in my nose, a sign my nostrils were filled with water. I gasped for air, spitting out bubbles of water as my head went underwater a second time.

Just moments before, I floated in peace. In a heartbeat, it was a war for survival—it was me against Goliath—a much stronger and potentially deadly opponent. I fought him with all my might—kicking my legs, pounding and slapping the water with my hands determined he wouldn't take me down. But my efforts were futile. My might was not enough. I needed something more. I was in desperate need of oxygen—rapidly inhaling and exhaling. When I bounced back above water, I could see and hear the laughter of the teenagers still playing about 20 or so yards away. One of the boys even looked at me as I tried to cry out, "Help! Help!" But he turned his attention back to playing with his friends.

A thousand voices raced through my mind, but the loudest said, "You're about to drown. You're going to die."

The knotted, multicolored rope came into view. It was the lifeline I needed to reach that separated me from the shallow water—but it was about eight or ten feet away. I could also make out the floats attached to the rope, spaced no more than four or five feet apart. If I could just reach them, I might be able to save myself. My rubber ducky had floated too far away.

When I went under the third time, exhausted from fighting, ingesting awful chemical-laced water and out of air, I remembered a television program I had recently watched. A swim expert was talking about the dangers of drowning. His number one rule was, "don't panic!"

I already flunked that test.

Second, was something about floating—your body will naturally float. However, mine was not. Then, I recalled his third warning. If you go down a third time and don't save yourself, you will drown.

Remembering those words, I knew I didn't have time to wait for someone to help me. I had to save myself. It wasn't a fair fight, but neither was David's battle. When armed with only a rock, he slew Goliath. But David didn't fight alone—God was on his side. I don't remember calling on the Lord, but I remembered the swimming expert saying, "If you don't have enough air, you will die. My survival skills must have kicked in by a God-sized miracle.

Suddenly, I left panic's door and started kicking my long legs and moving my arms like the Olympics swimmers I had watched a hundred times. I had no idea what I was doing or if it was correct. There was no method to my madness. I took long strokes, flipping my head side to side and using my arms to push back the water, trying to keep my body flat and head above water with my eyes razor-focused on the pools rope floatation line several feet away. I'm certain near-death desperation filled my eyes, and it still gives me chills when I think back to that day. I can't even remember breathing. I just recalled not accepting this would be the end of my life. God was not calling me home that day, and He came to my rescue. I know God showed up and strengthened my tired limbs and fearful soul to save me.

Isiah 35:4 (NIV) says, "to those with fearful hearts, 'Be strong, do not fear; your God will come, he will come with vengeance; with divine retribution he will come to save you.'"

After that near-death experience, I knew I needed to take swim lessons—I needed to trust that God was bigger than my fear and act accordingly. Instead, I became scared to death of the water to the point of anxiety attacks. I didn't venture into the pool again until a year after my near-drowning, but even then, I would only wade or stand in the waist-high section.

* * * *

The night before I packed for our eleven-day honeymoon on a gorgeous cruise ship to Tahiti, I pondered whether I should tell my new husband how panic-stricken I felt. We poured over so many brochures on exciting, warm getaways before we finally settled on the French Polynesian Island. Our travel agent said it had a reputation for romance, a place we could spend time luxuriating in the pleasure of each other, a peaceful place that was perfect for wedded bliss. Rodney was so looking forward to getting away. We both lived hectic lives and still had a commuter marriage since he was based in DC.

I didn't want to spoil it for him as I asked a lot of last-minute questions trying to calm my fear. "Are you sure we will dock and disembark at the port and step onto a boardwalk to dry land?"

"Yes, honey, that's what the travel agent told us. What's wrong? Are you nervous?"

"No, I'm just preparing, and you know the reporter in me. I like to know what's going to happen before it happens."

That was a lie. I was having nightmarish flashbacks of a trip to Aruba with a girlfriend and taking a 20-person tourist boat to a nearby party island. It looked like a 20 or 30 footer. She convinced me we wouldn't feel much turbulence since there were no rough seas, and we'd simply glide over to our destination, which was a quick ten-minute boat ride. I was reluctant since it was the first time I had ever been in the ocean in a small boat. When our private tour guide helped us on, eight or nine other passengers already had their seats, ready to depart. I immediately noticed the couple who sat in front of us. The mother bounced a handsome infant up and now on her lap. I will never forget his baby-blue eyes. They took on an incredible blueish, emerald hue, depending on how the Caribbean sunburst waters hit his face. He smiled at me, flapping his arms to his side in his life preserver. I asked the guide for a safety vest for myself. He gladly obliged even though no one else wore one. It was only Baby Blue and I decked out in our orange floatation attire. He sat toward the bow, or front part of the boat, and I was in the back near the stern.

As the last passengers boarded, my demeanor changed automatically. I was no longer listening and chatting with my girlfriend. I inhaled and exhaled slowly and deeply. As the small craft's engine started and the boat swayed a bit as it pulled away from the dock, I grabbed my girlfriend's knee with a lot of pressure.

"Ouch, Romona," she said. "It's okay—it's just a little movement as we taxi away. Relax."

"Alright," I responded softly. "It just freaked me out for a moment."

"You okay?"

"Yes, I just wasn't ready for it." I hoped it was true.

Then without warning, the boat seemed to jump from zero to 50 or 60 within seconds. My heart started racing, then pounded against my ribcage. Before I knew it, I literally hit the deck! I plopped down on all fours, my knees and both hands flat on the deck of the boat. I must have looked like an unbelievable mess—a tall woman in a beautiful multi-colored floor-length sundress, strapped in a life preserver, crouched on the floor.

My girlfriend bent over me, frantically trying to coax me back up in my seat. "Romona, Romona it's okay."

"Why is it rocking violently back in forth like this?" I yelled up at her.

"It's just a little turbulence as the boat tries to steady and balance itself in the water. Get back up here," she said, scolding me as if I were a child.

It was obvious to everyone, including the infant, that I needed help. When I managed to calm myself and look up, there was my little friend, his baby-blue eyes locked on me. His head moved so slowly from side-to-side, it looked like it was anatomically set to turn a half-an-inch every split second. The toddler's arms went straight up over his head while his body flattened as if he was trying to scoot down and climb out of his mother's arms and lap. The longer I stared at him, I realized my posture probably meant to him that I wanted to play piggyback, as I had done many times with my nieces and nephews. It was in a position we all recognized as kids. He wanted to jump down and play as he assumed I was doing, but his mom held him tightly in her lap.

Seeing how calm and unafraid that child was snapped me back to reality. My girlfriend's voice had become distant to me, even though she sat right next to me. All I could see was the juxtaposition of this baby who was fearless and me on the floor afraid of drowning. When he pointed and giggled at me, it was the therapy I needed. I grew brave and eased back up to the bench beside my friend. He literally clapped his hands together, erupting in a loud medley of baby babble as I emerged off the floor as if to say good job.

Packing for my honeymoon, remembering that unflattering day brought my fear of water back into focus. If a baby could do it, I could too.

* * * *

Our cruise ship, the Princess, arrived in the South Pacific. Before Rodney and I disembarked for the island, I went out on the deck off our bedroom suite at the back of the ship to get a quick glimpse of nature's breathtaking beauty. I loved watching the sky change from reddish-orange hues at sunrise to brilliant blues at midday. I remember the ocean's water being indescribable in color—at various times crystal blue, aqua, cobalt and turquoise. I spotted a family of dolphins during what looked like playtime, diving up and out of the water, and then disappearing for a few moments. I had exceptional, endless unobstructed views, an incredible front-row seat to their natural habitat.

A litany of colorful fish visible from my deck swam with ease. Off in the distance, massive, majestic mountain peaks and tropical jungles peered out at me, a reminder of the true beauty of untouched nature. The sound of the ocean waves danced atop the seas in the tropical breeze, some crashing against rocks ever so often.

I savored each and every spectacular view, soaking in the sun and beauty of the world around me, embracing the enchanting luxury my husband and I could afford. The visions seemed ethereal, almost heavenly, as they forced a calmness all over my body as if they transported me into another dimension. I'm not usually overly dramatic—but I truly felt the presence of God as I marveled at His creation.

In that moment, I dove into the ocean of God's grace and goodness in my life, thanking Him for allowing me to witness such an incredible experience. Growing up in rural Missouri, I never dreamed a trip like this would ever be possible.

The beautiful moment slammed to a halt when I realized we docked, but still floated in the middle of the ocean. I could see the island in the distance. My fear overtook the certainty of God's goodness. Trying not to show my trembling, I questioned Rodney about why we were so far away from shore.

"Oh, the ship is too large to dock at the port, so we have to take a tender to the island. It is a really short ride."

"But why?" My voice shook.

"When docking is not an option for a cruise ship, it will anchor in the deeper water out here offshore, and then we take smaller boats to get to shore," he explained lovingly.

"What's a tender?"

"It's just a small boat that will transport us to shore. Remember, our travel agent told us about them."

"No, I don't recall." I'd been so focused on the whole trip and the excursions. "How small? How many people does it hold? One hundred, two hundred? How big is it?"

My questions fired, fast and furious, as my heart rate elevated, and my anxiety level increased rapidly.

I could tell my responses concerned Rodney. He explained again, trying to calm me. "Honey, some ports are shallower than others, so it would be tricky, almost impossible, for the ship to navigate and dock at port, so we have to take this smaller boat."

I tried focusing on the fact that I was on my honeymoon with the man I waited for and wasn't going be rattled by the water. But it was easier said than done. Goliath towered again, blocking my path. Only this time it was not in a pool, but an ocean! I was no match for this giant, six-hundred miles long, thirteen-thousand feet deep ocean. He had the advantage. After all, I was on his turf. Sure, he looked harmless enough, but not knowing how to swim, and our ship perched on the open seas, I didn't stand a chance against this powerful, frightening giant that could swallow me whole if I fell in! Moments before, the ocean reminded of me of God's goodness, but no more. Fear commanded full control.

As The Princess crewmembers helped us disembark and board the tender, I tried to remember I was going to be okay. I felt safe with Rodney. He was a strong swimmer and promised not to let anything happen to me. He assured me I would not and could not fall overboard.

The enclosed tender offered protection from any rain and other elements. The passengers smiled at me, making me feel comfortable, asking where we were from, and conversations about Cleveland helped take my mind off the fact I was sitting atop miles of water. The tender could hold maybe 50 to 100 people, and there were only 30 or 40 of us.

When the boat's engine revved up and started to push away from our giant, floating, majestic hotel, the anxiety kicked in at high speed. Normal breathing increased at a rapid pace. The temperatures in the upper 80s started to feel like 100 degrees. I smelled the saltwater and imagined it filling my nostrils as my head sank below the water.

I started to talk to myself softly but loud enough that Rodney asked, "What honey? What did you say?"

"Nothing," I replied. "I was just thinking aloud."

I rubbed my hands together, caressed my palms, forced my hair behind my ears, and bounded my knees up and down continuously in motion. I was about to have an emotional outburst. I could feel Goliath coming for me, and I had no coping skill I could use to fight him.

When the tender flipped slightly to one side to steady itself, I lost it, letting out a loud scream and grabbing Rodney violently by the arm, "Help me!"

Passengers gawked and eyeballed me. Most looked so concerned, but I recall hearing a woman whisper, "If she's afraid of water what is she doing out here in the middle of nowhere?" At the moment, I couldn't worry about what other people thought of my hysteria. I was in a panic-filled trance and needed help.

Rodney reeled in utter shock, holding me tightly, trying to reassure his new bride we were safe and not going to drown. I rocked back and forth, begging him to hold me tighter and help me. I never looked into his eyes, but I could tell Rodney was at a loss for how to comfort me.

Suddenly, I felt a hand at my back and one on my shoulder. I jumped. A man who was sitting behind us said he was a doctor. He instructed me to breathe.

"Miss, calm down," he said to me then addressed Rodney. "What's her name?"

"Romona," Rodney replied, likely glad for some assistance.

His firm voice demanded obedience. "Romona, I'm a doctor. You're having an anxiety attack. Take deep breaths."

I began to relax at the sound of his soothing, reassuring voice.

"That's right, deep breaths. Slow, in and out. You're safe." As I shakily tried to follow his instructions, he continued, "Think about your husband. Raise your head, look at him and breathe calmly. Nothing is going to happen to you. We're all here."

My face was buried in Rodney's shoulder. I started to breathe more normally, and eventually, we reached land.

"Thank you," I murmured without turning to acknowledge the doctor. I was in no shape to talk to anyone. Rodney turned to thank him and exchanged quick pleasantries.

As we went about our day, shopping and sightseeing, I realized with certainty, this was not a fair fight. How could I confront my fear of water in his enormous territory? Even Rodney and I, combining our strength, weren't enough to conquer my fear.

I then remembered no opponent is greater than God. He was my powerful protector. When I prayed, I could lean on His strength and mercy to fight the battles I couldn't. I finally realized I had a choice—I could continue to run from my fear, or I could face it head-on with His love and power. No matter how big the fear, God is enough.

I vowed during my honeymoon in paradise that I would take down my Goliath by taking back the power I'd given the giant. I allowed fear to keep me hostage from enjoying my love of sun and sand and beaches. I was sick of sitting on the sidelines while my husband and everyone else enjoyed the good life and all the luxuries that came with it. Rodney went snorkeling without me. He went deep-sea scuba diving without me. He swam in some of the most beautiful waters I've ever seen without me. He took a private helicopter ride over some of the most incredible lush tropics ever created—without me.

I stayed back on the hot, steamy beach, hunkered down under a huge umbrella with a drink, doodling sketches in the sand and tossing sand between my feet and toes to entertain myself as I waited for my husband and the other fun people to get back from an amazing adventure on the seas. Don't get me wrong. Hanging out on the beautiful sands of Tahiti with an umbrella drink is nothing to sneeze at—but I let fear sandbag my happiness and priceless memories with my husband.

I declared, "No more!"

As soon as I got back home to Cleveland, I would slay my Goliath!

The two of us would meet four months later in a community pool where I took swim lessons for adult beginners. Recalling my first swim lesson still emotes memories of high drama. My swim instructor and seven or so senior classmates had the patience of Job. They helped to gradually coax me to submerge my head underwater. I remember trembling, eyes wide as she placed both of her hands on my shoulders, helping to lower my 5-foot

10-inch body under five feet of water. The pool's water would get to my neck, and I'd spring back up. She tried dipping me down, and repeatedly, when it reached my chin, I stood straight up.

"Baby steps, Romona," she assured me. "We're going to go at your pace."

I prayed for several weeks prior to my lessons, asking God to be my guide. I needed His reassurances I would not drown. Each day, I drew strength from trusting the people He surrounded me with. I learned so much more about swimming during that six-week class—the innate goodness of people who want you to succeed, willing to allow the disruption of their lessons to provide security and comfort to an obvious fright-filled student.

Learning to swim was a lot like growing your faith. Once I relaxed and trusted the person in charge, knowing she and the others would not allow any harm to come to me, I was able to walk into the water like the Lord instructed Peter. I started to have faith I wouldn't drown and could finally immerse my entire body underwater myself and follow instructions. If you could see the smile produced when I floated for the first time, swam a lap, raced my instructor and practiced holding my breath underwater for several minutes!

Two years later, I had learned to swim and checked off box number seven on my bucket list—swim with the dolphins. In deep water swimming alongside God's creation, they dove underneath, lifted my body a few inches, and tossed me forwarded. I will never forget that most incredible experience of my life.

I slew my Goliath, thanks to God's grace and my willingness to trust him.

What I've Learned...
A Battle Plan against Self-doubt

"Our doubts are traitors, and make us lose the good we oft might win, by fearing to attempt."

- William Shakespeare

I wasted so many years of being afraid, doubting my ability to ever learn to swim.

We will always suffer bouts of self-doubt and fear in some form or fashion—some bigger than others.

Doubt can be a crippling and persuasive voice that holds us back from achieving our dreams. It can keep us stuck in our comfort zone, preventing us from making needed changes. If we're not aware of the enemies' voice, it can attach itself and never leave us alone. It resembles that annoying person you wish would take a hint and leave. It pushes you to have gut-wrenching honest talks with yourself. But what if we cut the cord with daily feelings of uncertainty and fear? What if we could take on life's challenges, pray bolder, stronger and more meaningful prayers, and trust God with our whole heart and our destiny? I am living proof you can have your mind renewed through the Word of God.

My heart and mind feel absolutely equipped to handle that haunting fear, anxiety and doubt when it rears its ugly head in my life—because I know that it's not my power versus fear's brawn. It's God's power, and His power is more than enough to conquer fear. I slew my Goliath, but I've had hundreds of bouts with fear and second-guessing myself that threatened to detour God's planned destination. I was being controlled by thoughts in my head that caused me to doubt my own power. I now start by speaking the fear out of existence out loud. Self-doubt is much like fear, a lack of faith. It is not all bad either. Sometimes, doubt is a voice that alerts you and causes pause if a situation is not right for you. It's critical to know who's speaking to you.

When I am inundated by discouraging voices, I first try to figure out where the negative thoughts come from. Are they my own voice or those of the enemy? I always practice self-talk to myself when conflicted, believing God loves me and hears me. I talk to the Lord, asking for His protection and what it is He would have me do. Other times, I'll call a prayer-warrior friend and share my inner thoughts or grab my "go-to" scriptures about fear and doubt and repeat them over and over.

Doubt will speak lies to you, telling you how things will turn out. You have to fight it with faith, which will show you the truth—God is strong enough to beat any enemy, and He won't leave your side.

It can be a never-ending battle. When you are over one problem, something else arises. At times, you might wonder if this is all there is—every day, waking up and looking forward to another day of fighting fear? Not at all, God wants us to be joyous, to go on vacation, take walks in the park, go to the movies and dinners with our friends—even swim in His beautifully created ocean. He keeps fighting your battles alongside you. He'll never leave, and He always wins.

A Battle Plan against Loneliness

Most people think when a woman says she's lonely, she's automatically seeking male companionship. However, I have nine sisters and several female friends, and I know being lonely for them means several different things. Sure, a few want a relationship, but others just want a connection, shared interests, a companion to see a movie or have dinner, a road trip buddy. A serious relationship and marriage, even a healthy one, isn't the cure for loneliness.

You might look at pics on Instagram and think everyone is having fun but you, everyone has a special someone, and no one's lonely but you. It's the lie that binds. It feeds on your insecurity and confirms how you already feel about yourself. Isolation and rejection can make you feel lonely. You can have a partner and still feel alone. You can be in a room full of people and still feel lonely.

The Lord God said, "It is not good for the man to be alone. I will make a helper suitable for him." (Genesis 2:18 NIV)

The enemy wants you to believe you will always be alone. You become depressed and isolate yourself from family, friends and definitely strangers. In those times, you have to break free of the mental bondage holding you hostage and create a battle plan.

Scripture says joy cometh in the morning, but you have to help create that happiness in your life. It starts by taking the first step. Push yourself out of your comfort zone, and use your alone *time to discover talents you might have or missed opportunities that could bring you joy and fulfillment.*

You know the basic stuff you've grown tired of hearing. Go out to the mall, a bookstore, the grocery store, smile, and say hello to a stranger. Try striking up a conversation with someone new at church. Pursue your interests or hobbies or take up new ones. Instead of wallowing in boredom and sadness, try making new friends. Join a gym, a club, take a class or become a member of an organization. Grab a good book or your favorite magazine, and instead of reading at home, go a local spot where you can be in the presence of people. The World Wide Web has become a giant cure for loneliness. Talking to people online and on social media is a great way to battle loneliness because you can stay in a safe, comfortable space and still have contact with the outside world. I have reconnected with old classmates and colleagues, and I enjoy new acquaintances.

But life behind a computer doesn't fulfill the need for human contact.

I told you earlier I swore a life of celibacy for two years while I waited for God to send me a suitable mate—no dates, no romance, no intimate contact or conversations with a man, and it was great! I'm serious. I didn't know it then, but I truly needed the time to get to know me.

I stayed busy, hanging out and traveling with friends. But during those quiet moments, when it was just my thoughts and me, I learned a lot about myself. What I wanted in a mate, how I needed to change and prepare myself when God said I was ready. I was plagued by scary voices during my waiting period. Some thoughts distorted the truth, telling me I could and should go out with suitors, even when my inner voice whispered warning signs I should not. The enemy's voice filled my mind with lies that I was nearing 40, and I might as well take the slim pickins' at the moment because all of the good men were taken.

Politicians, entertainers and professional athletes asked me out on dates, and each time, the voice of God said no. Like any good reporter, I learned to do my homework, knowing things aren't always as they seem. Money and status don't always equal faithfulness and a lifetime commitment. So, I waited. I ignored my longing for a mate and focused on putting my faith in God, believing He knows what's best.

I get it. It is so much easier to make friends when we're kids. Saying hello to a total stranger, as an adult, can create anxiety, inciting your heart to jump out of your chest if they don't reciprocate the kindness. And yes, people might reject you. I can recall a couple of times I was getting in some shopping therapy in the Big Apple. I'd walk along 5th Avenue, in and out of stores in New York, and would say a simple hello to passersby. You would think I had a contagious plague from the sharp looks of "who are you?" and "why are you saying hello to me?" After all, I am too important to press my lips together, form a smile and open my mouth to be polite. It made me laugh over how important they thought they were, but for others, it can be a crushing blow to their confidence.

Some things and situations are uncomfortable for us. You may not be one person's cup of tea, but you could be a breath of fresh air for another. Nevertheless, human contact is essential.

A study found that when seniors are socially isolated, there is an increased risk of an earlier death, by as much as 26 percent. Loneliness is widespread. Three out of every four Americans reported bouts of loneliness, researchers found. Wisdom appeared to be a strong factor in avoiding feelings of loneliness. People who had empathy, compassion and control over their emotions were much less likely to feel lonely.

The days we have left on this earth are precious moments that should not be wasted wallowing in self-pity.

The fear of loneliness can often force you into a relationship with the wrong person. It's unfortunate, but peers, family and society, in general, create enormous pressure to be in a relationship, get married, or have someone in our life. If not, you can be made to somehow feel less whole.

We all cope with feelings of being unwanted in different ways. Some of us smile, but we want to cry. We talk, but we're suffering in silence. We pretend to be happy, but on the inside, the loneliness has broken our spirit.

I can hear your thoughts as you read this chapter—yeah, Romona. You are a journalist with probably dozens of friends and live an exciting life. How does someone like me who is not a well-known celebrity and has few friends cope with feelings of being unloved and unwanted?

It's the power of the voice inside you. Don't contaminate your mind with ugly thoughts about yourself. Instead, be gentle and kind with yourself and work to discover why you choose to abuse yourself mentally. Sometimes, the worst thing you can do when you're lonely is to listen to the debilitating voices in your head.

It's a battle no one can help you with. Loneliness has to be fought by you. Being alone will force you to take a deeper look at who you are. If you enjoy you, others will too.

Don't give up. Don't lose your passion for life. God has a plan for you, and He loves you every step of the way. He will send people into your life to show you His love.

Chapter 7

UNMASKING YOUR FEAR

"I have learned over the years that when one's mind is made up, this diminishes fear; knowing what must be done does away with fear."

- Rosa Parks

We all applaud the bravery of the first lady of Civil Rights, Rosa Parks, as she was called. The courage it took to push past her fear, take a stand and refuse to vacate her seat for a white passenger, which sparked the Montgomery Bus Boycott.

Notice in her quote that she learned what she did about fear *over the years*.

Overcoming and slaying this giant emotion called fear can take time.

Just because you trust in God and have faith doesn't mean you don't fear. It takes a lot of work to find your own strength, your own voice and not be defined by other people's opinion of you.

When unexpected circumstances shake us to the core, it's only natural to feel afraid and uncertain. But what if we could learn to trade in our anxiety for the certainty that God's plans are good?

"Trust in the LORD with all your heart and lean not on your own understanding; in all your ways submit to him, and he will make your paths straight. Do not be wise in your own eyes; fear the LORD and shun evil." (Proverbs 3:5-7 NIV)

There is comfort in knowing God is ever-present in times of fear. He is never blind to our tears or deaf to our cries for help. He hears us, sees us and will save us. We just have to trust Him with all our hearts. God will keep you on track, on the right path. Fear is the silent enemy that keeps us from reaching our God-given potential. Our faith is planted in the truth of who God knows you are.

Have ever found yourself asking God to help you out of a situation, only not to wait on Him but trying to go ahead of Him and solve the problem yourself? In most cases, when I went it alone, I failed.

Some of us allow the voices of fear to control us and guide us every day.

I believe fear, with its many masks, holds a grain of truth about us, and we fear being found out. We've learned to live with fear through the image we project to the world. Masking ourselves has become part of our everyday existence. We breathe it, speak it, and live it—until the jolt of it is tolerable.

We have to start looking at fear for what it is. Fear is a scam, a con, a liar that can bring about a world of hurt in your life if you don't learn to fight back. I feel an invisible shield surrounds my life, helping repel demons that try to infiltrate my mind, block my plan and steal my happiness. Evidence that you fear God can be seen by the way you live your life.

> *"The remarkable thing about God is that when you fear God, you fear nothing else, whereas if you do not fear God, you fear everything else."*
>
> – Oswald Chambers

Fearing God keeps us on the straight and narrow. As a teenager, when I would go out, my mom warned me she couldn't see what I was up to—but God sees all. Those words put the "fear of God" in me! I always felt His presence watching me. I found myself apologizing when I did things that weren't Christian-like, fearing He would punish me harshly.

And, the Bible tells us we should fear God.

"The fear of the Lord is the beginning of knowledge; fools despise wisdom and instruction." (Proverbs 1-7 NIV)

Some small fears are just built-in from our childhood, and we're not even aware it is there. I can chomp down on fried chicken or a lamb chop and a seared marbled steak at record speeds. It is habit. I have always eaten as if it was my last meal, fearing starvation. My childhood experiences of not having enough nourishment stuck with me into adulthood. I remember gathering around a table with 11 kids and 1 chicken to feed us all. Now I can afford all the food I need, and eating fast isn't good for me, especially red meat. My acid reflux quickly confirms that truth shortly after the meal if I don't take small bites and chew slowly. So I had to learn to slow down and know that there was more food. I was not going to starve.

How come we can't use that same analogy with God's Word? Why don't we tell ourselves just because we've always done it that way, doesn't mean we can't change?

Now I deal with everyday challenges by feeding my mind with healthy doses of faith and knowing God will not let me go without what I need.

Fear in my life diminished greatly because my faith grew tremendously—because I trust God unequivocally. I am no longer afraid to tell friends I need a boost, I'm feeling depressed, I'm concerned about a problem, or I need a break.

Fear doesn't bring out the best in you—instead, it hinders your progress, lying to you about what is and what will be. Fear can be bargained with, wrestled with, but ultimately, one way or another you will have to deal with unmasking it and take control of your life again. It's time to stop being stuck in your comfort zone, fantasizing about breaking free but cornered by your fear. Ironically, the best way to break free comes in the form of surrender.

If we don't surrender to God, anxiety constantly fuels fear.

Years ago, I met a colleague for lunch. As we exchanged pleasantries about our lives, she abruptly halted the conversation.

"Excuse me for a minute. I need to pop this Xanax. My anxiety spirals out of control when I'm worried."

"I hope that's a prescription," I chimed in. "What's wrong? I hate to say it, but you don't look so good. Are you sleeping?

"Romona, I needed to talk to you," she whispered with a bit of hysteria in her voice. She breathed heavily and ran her hands through her freshly done silky locks. Normally she exuded confidence, but not today. "I've been going crazy. My contract is up this month, and they haven't even started to talk to me about a new deal yet. Do you think that means they won't sign me? Do you think I'm gonna be fired? Should I be looking elsewhere?"

"Girl, with all of our talks about 'faith and the assurance of things we hope for,' you are having a panic attack, right now in front of me? Really?"

"I know, Romona, but you are stronger than me. Contract time is so stressful for me. I always fear I won't be renewed."

I tried easing her worry by dishing out quick bits of paraphrased scriptures, like "trouble don't come but for a season," or "God will direct your path," and "remember God is in charge."

Nothing I said registered. She floated between delirium and distress, constantly flipping her hair, pulling the ends of it and pressing me for concrete assurances about what she should do if managers didn't present her with a contract offer soon.

No matter how I tried to comfort her, she seemed satisfied with being in a space of fear and not leaning on the Word of God, which says, "I will prosper you and not harm, and give you hope and a future." (Jeremiah 29:11)

Being in a state of fear is all she's ever known. Her faith in God does not allow her to jump, to take the leap of faith and trust that the Lord will provide a net to catch her below. To overcome fear, we must not only know God's truth, but we also have to follow it. We have to act in accordance with what the Bible says is true.

She later was signed to a new contract and went back to being an outwardly confident journalist.

It is not easy to deal with the unknown road ahead when you're going through a tough spell. The devil masks himself in every emotion you feel, and he feeds on that worry and anxiety. That's why it's critical you recognize his tactics.

If my friend had given her fear to God, He could have transformed the situation.

Seeking help from a therapist, and maybe medication, is crucial if you need someone to help you get to the bottom of what's plaguing you and keeping you trapped in a state of panic. The fear of losing everything you built through a job loss can be devastating. I know. I've lived it. It's even harder to share with others how much you're suffering because of unexpected problems that turn your life upside down.

But God has to be your "go-to" in times of trouble—no matter what.

My friend knows she's living a life of emotional fear—she is the wizard of worrying. She readily admits her emotions are out of whack! She reacts to any bad news with a high level of intensity, which causes her to seek comfort in her meds to calm her nerves instead of turning to the Word of God. We've talked about how she's allowed those negative feelings to dominate, and at times, cripple her. She internalizes the fear so deeply, the pain just sits there, and her anxiety builds. She tells me she reads the Word, and she believes.

So why do some of us plug into problems and not the power of God?

Have you ever wondered how some people have such great faith that they remain calm and steady no matter what life throws at them? You don't see them worrying or stressed, and if they do, it is momentary. What is the difference in their heart, in their mindset, in their daily practices?

For me, it was spiritual growth. Throughout the years, I learned to keep God first in my life.

Earlier, when I was spiritually immature, fear was part of my everyday existence. I focused on the harsh circumstances. I accepted the Lord as my Savior because it was something my parent told me I had to do. Even though I believed, I had faint faith. I didn't have an unwavering belief that if I fell, God would always be there to catch me. I hoped and prayed he would, but that voice of doubt questioned His presence. I had to grow my faith, and that meant pushing past the emotional instability in my life.

You know you're growing your faith when that mental circuit breaker in your head is rewired, and you react to bad news in a different way, at least sometimes. Bad news no longer automatically throws you into a state of shock, and unchecked emotions don't paralyze you with fear.

I now live a more-confident, less-worried life. I'm not fearless or always free from worry. I just deal with it differently now. Often times when unexpected bad surprises come my way, I sit down, take a few deep breaths, pray, grab a cup of coffee, and say, "Okay, I am going to tackle this."

Case in point, I got a huge, unexpected tax bill this year. I've always received a refund. I won't lie. I did scream at the gigantic number and cursed our lawmakers, but only for a second. I called a friend to share the news, seeking some comfort and encouragement, only to find out she too was hit with a whopping bill. We both had a great laugh, offered each other some wise advice, and lightened the conversation with something positive in our lives. Some days, you have to cut through the clutter of fear and worry and reconnect with the fight later. That payment could wait until tax day, but obsessing about it could only ruin a perfectly good day.

We are all wired differently. There is no single way to handle fear, but the day I declared I would no longer allow something or someone to steal my peace through fear and anger was the day I started to truly live. God loves all of his children. He doesn't love me anymore than He loves you. He's just waiting for you to know that. He wants you to get on board with changing your life. He wants you to start living by faith and not sight or appearances. What you see can be deceiving. Stop letting your emotions dictate how you wake up and start your day. Recognize the little triggers that set you off and allow fear to creep in, then tell them the truth of God. Breaking old habits is tough. Sometimes, we need to hit the reset button and use a different approach and reaction to problems.

Fear is a formidable opponent—I've fought it—winning more times than not when I allowed God to enter the ring. Millions of people wake up every day and operate in a space of fear. It lies at the root of many of life's problems.

So often, women are made to feel fear is a weakness and guilt sets in. We suffer from perfection, rejection, anxiety—fearing failure and not measuring up. Some are drowning in depression, loss and pain. The worry of being alone can feed on our vulnerability and insecurity. We're crippled by tremendous stress during a struggle, unsure of brighter days.

While you cry out why me, know there is a reason God's sending you through the storm. It's your testimony, your test. He's trying to grow your faith and draw you closer to Him.

When you know God's speaking an idea or plan into existence for your life, you can't let anything hold you back. Announce to fear you are done—it will no longer hold you back. Declare that you are finished second-guessing yourself. Stop beating yourself up over past mistakes, letting guilt and the haunting of the past hold you back from what God created you to be. Stop fighting God's purpose in your life.

What I've Learned... Living Scared

In all my conversations with people I interviewed, I realized for some people, thoughts of fear and despair is all they've ever known. They didn't get an equal or head start. They started nine, ten steps back, most living through unimaginable pain. Broken dreams, busted plans. They didn't get to choose their parents. Some were abandoned, raised in unstable environments as children, fighting through the pain of raising themselves or being tossed from one foster home to another, suffering abuse and neglect. They didn't have the means to get in the best schools or pay for tutoring because homelessness left them behind in school.

But the life they were dealt didn't stop them from daring to dream big. When most people told them, "You can't do it, you don't have what it takes," they pushed on.

I recall a conversation with a young lady at Nordstrom's a few years ago. She was a five-foot ball of energy in the shoe department. She also flashed a smile and greeted you with a sweet hello as warm and satisfying as your favorite morning latte. I would watch her tend to three or four clients at a time, scurrying to the back room to grab shoe sizes and onto the showroom floor at record speeds as to not keep her customers waiting. I complimented her on her work ethic.

She said, "Thank you, but I won't be here long. I got another job." She swallowed deep, finding it difficult to hold back her joy.

She went on to confide that she had a college degree and couldn't find a job in her field, accounting, so she gave up trying. She grew content that her department-store job paid the bills, allowing her to take care of her daughter. She lived scared for several years, unable to find an accounting job. She heard so many rejections she started to believe the lies Satan told her about herself. Even though she had an associate degree, she was still tied to memories of homelessness and abuse in foster care. The many job rejections left her with feelings of being unwanted, unworthy and not good enough all over again. She started to believe the ugliness her foster parents said about her—that she was stupid, didn't deserve good breaks and would never be successful.

She stopped looking for career jobs—until she waited on a customer who just happened to head an accounting firm. The woman was so impressed by her delightful disposition that they struck up a conversation about her job. That conversation, over shoes, led to a job interview and a new job in her field of study.

God has the power to remove every obstacle, and He loves you. When you depend on Him, even when life doesn't look good, He will be there.

The Bible says in Isaiah 61:7 (NIV), "Instead of your shame, you will receive a double portion, and instead of disgrace you will rejoice in your inheritance. And so you will inherit a double portion in your land, and everlasting joy will be yours."

God is a powerful God. He can pay you back double for the trouble you've endured. You are not the only one going through failure. Your walk may be different than mine, but failure has visited my doorstep and threatened to deter my dreams. However, my success depended on how I reacted to it. Be careful. Misery loves company.

I learned to eliminate fakery, buffoonery and phoniness in my space. I now wear my own shoes and walk through my God-led journey, authentically me. I'm not afraid to fail; it's just one more lesson to keep trying and learning until I get it right.

People, who thought they were doing you wrong, actually set you up for a testimony you would not otherwise have. I have always come out the victor when I allowed Him in the ring. And, when I didn't win, I still never lost because the outcome wasn't for me.

Failure is not Fatal

The fear of failure can be daunting and scary, but applying God's grace and prayer, and waiting for His timing, has done amazing things for me.

Life isn't always fair. It can be frightening and sometimes, it will hand you some crap. I hate that word, but it's true. You can get dumped on through no fault of your own, and it feels awful. You climb out of it only to have something else knock you down. How do you handle the mental pressures when things fall apart? Trust in God and have faith.

When the difficult times come, we question why God hasn't arrived. Every time I faced a storm in my life—job loss, infertility, sexual harassment—I implored God to show up. I questioned what was taking so long. Why hadn't he come to my rescue?

What do you do when you're in the midst of the failure, and God's timing seems questionable, His lack of intervention is painful, and His promises doubtful? I had to learn in His timing, not mine.

God wants credit, glory. He wants you to tell someone what He did, and it wasn't by chance or luck. I hear people say all the time, "My, I was lucky. That car almost hit me head-on" or "just my luck that tumor is benign." I know a miraculous recovery or near miss on the highway is God stepping in saying, "It is not your time child, I still have work for you."

Nothing God does is by accident in the midst of your troubles. He stopped the sun for Joshua when he was chasing his enemies, He protected Daniel from hungry lions, and He rescued Joseph, who then became second in command in Egypt. These are Bible stories, but for me, He delivered me from poverty to prosperity when I followed His path. He saved my career when I thought it was over. When failed relationships left me lonely and bewildered, He showed me what true love looks and feels like.

We all fail and live imperfect lives. We make mistakes, and I believe that is the beginning of wisdom. When we start to recondition our minds about failure, we see it not as a bad word, but as a lesson toward our greatness.

I have never faced a challenge expecting to fail. I've done my homework and prepared myself for the possible bumps in the road and the what if's. But I never focused on the failure aspect. You can embrace it, learn from it and move on.

Life can often look so very different than we hoped or expected. Some failures simply catch us off guard for a moment, but others shatter us completely. We feel disappointed and disillusioned, and we quietly start to wonder if there will ever be brighter days.

"Praise be to the God and Father of our Lord Jesus Christ, the Father of compassion and the God of all comfort, who comforts us in all our troubles so that we can comfort those in any trouble with the comfort we ourselves receive from God." (2 Corinthians 1: 3-4 NIV)

During troubled times, you've got to be able to keep going, even when the voices in your head say you can't. That's when you draw on deep reserves of energy to go the distance—knowing He is always there.

Remember, failure is not fatal. It's just a setback. Don't run from it, as hard as it is. Many successful people will tell you they failed dozens of times. In order to succeed in a career or new business venture, you have to have a tolerance for risk and not live afraid to fail.

When I decided I wanted to write books, I knew I was going to focus and put all of my passion in my writing. I worked day and night pouring my heart and soul into my work. I remember sending my first book to New York publishing houses and spending months querying multiple hotshot agents. I received so many rejection letters I lost count. I felt like a literary failure. I thought my manuscript had the workings of a moving and meaningful masterpiece that could motivate and inspire people, but none of them were interested. I won't lie. It stung!

I sent it to several national celebrities, and no one wrote back, even those I had met. I remember reacting to the rejection by burying my face in the bottom of an ice-cream carton with barbecue potatoes chips crushed inside it. (It might sound gross, but trust me the sweet and salty is heavenly.) The sugar-filled, high-sodium delight satisfied and soothed my then fragile ego and feelings of failure. Those carbs were just the right ingredient I needed, though a temporary fix, to boost my energy and confidence that despite the rejection, I could still be a successful author. They just weren't my path. I turned to God for my acceptance and assurances. In Him and the Word, I found the courage to continue following His roadmap.

"Therefore, since we are surrounded by such a great cloud of witnesses, let us throw off everything that hinders and the sin that so easily entangles. And let us run with perseverance the race marked out for us. (Hebrews 12:1-2 NIV)

The words of Hebrew were telling me not to quit, stay on the open road He mapped out for me. It was God's voice that spoke to me and said continue until I reached the finish line. I had to remember to keep my eyes on Jesus, the pioneer and perfecter of faith.

It's tough when your faith is flagging after a failure. You hear the Christian bumper sticker slogans or all the familiar clichés. The ones like, "God is in charge," we learn from our mistakes," "never give up," or "failure is simply a price we pay to achieve success."

I was looking at my perceived failure all wrong. I hoped having a big agent backing me would be a huge platform to boost my literary success and help me serve more people. But once I got over my fear of being seen as a literary flop, which had me paralyzed and stunted my writing for weeks, I realized I didn't need them to validate whether I had a good book. It was up to the reader. So, I decided to self-publish and take my book straight to the important people God wanted me to write for (you)!

I would write every day, pouring my heart, soul, reputation, and everything else into launching my first book. I was determined not to let the discouraging voices of a few stop me in my tracks.

When you wrestle with worry and become wracked with anxiety over problems in life, you only make yourself sick. Prolonged stress can literally kill you. It's also important not to do as I did. Don't internalize and personalize the failure and let it sit in the core of your being. I had to be pragmatic in a powerful way that God set me on this journey, and I could not, and would not, hightail it and run and give up at the first sign of trouble.

You can't always have a Plan B in case of failure. You can be hit over the head with the shock of your life. How you recover is up to you. You can't feel like that one bad interview was the end of the road, and you are doomed for any kind of career in the future. Your job suddenly downsizes, your name is called, and you receive that pink slip. How will you react? Will you allow the news to sink you into a slow depression-like quicksand, preventing you from moving forward? Will you become mired in anger, embarrassment, frustration, and self-recriminations, blaming yourself? Or will you start fighting to live another day, face the hand dealt to you, and allow it to spark a spiritual focus on what God is trying to teach you through the storm hitting you? God does things in His timing, not yours, and when you don't wait upon the Lord, you allow fear, not faith, to reign over your life.

Chapter 8

FEARLESS FAITH

Wheels spinning and whirring—the unmistakable humming, grinding, and squealing noise when your tires are stuck in the snow pervaded the interior of the car. Burning rubber from the tires emitted a disgusting noxious smell and added fog to already low visibility. Peering out the window, a postcard-picturesque setting of the enviable winter wonderland should leave me contented and peaceful. Snow covered everything around us, the entire two-lane country road where we were stuck, blanketed in the white stuff. The barren cornfield and soybean fields hid beneath the layers. Even the naked trees donned a suit of white. Fat, fluffy, falling snowflakes and icy breezes obliterated any doubt—we had landed in the middle of Snowmageddon, a full-fledged snowstorm.

A single light pole wrapped in white stood about 16 or 20 feet away, permitting a hint of light. The only visible sign of life outside our car on Route 2 in tiny Diehlstadt, Missouri was my mom. The sporadic whiteout conditions, produced by intermittently blowing snow and below-freezing temperatures, confirmed my fear.

We were in deep trouble.

I was 18 years old, sitting behind the wheel, terrified. We had no cell phones, and only the wealthiest people owned car phones in the 80s. The nearest gas station in the rural town sat two miles back on the desolate country road. The 150 people who lived there lived in scattered homes surrounded by acres of land. There was no sign of another vehicle on the scarcely traveled back road that provided a 15-minute short cut to our home in Wilson City.

The gas gauge still showed half a tank, more than enough to make the 25 miles to our house—if we didn't use it all trying to free ourselves from this dire situation.

Even though the dark terrified me, I coyly offered to walk back to the gas station to get help, hoping mom would reject the idea, and she did.

Mom knew it was no place for a teenage girl alone at night. She was also not willing to leave my sister and I stuck on a dark road. There was no way for the three of us to make the trek to get help. Melissa would never make it that far. Increasing the urgency, Mom knew my other siblings waited at home with my teenage sister. We were two hours late—they would be worried.

Through the snow and dim light, Mom's wide-eyed, crazed look peered at me from in front of her early 60s' Chevy. Hunched over, popping the hood, I assumed she wanted to find the cause of the engine running rough. She slammed the top down and began pushing the vehicle backward, rocking it back and forth with all her might, yelling for me to floor it in reverse. I floored the pedal to the point smoke filled the area around the car. I fearfully watched Momma absorb the pain as she strapped her body like a human shield in front of the car, time and time again trying to free us as she yelled for me to continue pushing the pedal to the metal.

"Romona, turn the wheels completely straight," she yelled at me. "Now, when I say go, mash the gas pedal down hard and keep it straight back. Don't cut your wheel."

Every time I drove the accelerator into the floor, the arrow on the speedometer went from zero to 60 like a high-speed jet racing down the runway before takeoff, but we got nowhere.

Our Chevy was sleek and white. We called it the Batmobile car because of the batwings on the back. The wing-shaped tail fins mimicked those on Batman and Robin's car, infatuating us. That thing felt like it weighed as much as a tank or an armored vehicle. It sported a hardtop with lots of silver metal on the front and back and a long silver stripe along the sides.

We could thank the Lord our tailpipe was free of snow, which meant we could run the heat to keep warm. We were also thankful for the car's flashers because the sometimes-blinding snow made the car almost invisible against the piles of frozen whiteness.

Mom would push and then jump back in the car to heat her bare hands, exposed in the freezing temperatures.

That night, she wore the nice coat reserved only for church or special outings. It was a gray, wool, knee-length coat with black specks, double-breasted with six large, black buttons. She had no scarf, no hat and no gloves or boots on—items considered luxuries, not necessities she could afford on her minimum-wage factory job. She wore her nice flat slip-on black leather shoes with wool socks under black slacks with a white shirt, which is what she mostly traveled in. I couldn't see them, though I had images of her feet sinking into the ankle-deep snow, freezing and wet. Her pant leg must have been equally drenched and extremely uncomfortable in what Mother Nature had served up.

We had nothing in the trunk that could help us—no salt, no dirt, no shovel, no flashlight or safety kit. We had a few plastic bags stuffed near the front of the trunk, and a window scraper, but they were tough to see since the only trunk's light was not functional.

Mom tried using the scraper and her bare hands clawing and digging the snow and ice away from the tires. I watched her from the driver's seat behind the wheel. Bent over, she desperately and frantically tried to free up a few feet in front of and behind the tires to free us.

I have never forgotten what I witnessed that night—a mother's love—a woman who would do anything to save her kids.

Through the closed windows, I heard Momma talking aloud to herself and God. "Lawd, help me. Help me and my chirrens," she repeated continuously. "Don't let us freeze to death out here."

Desperation glowed in Mom's eyes that night, but never any fear—purely sheer determination. Fear was no match for a mother's love. If panic crept in, she masked it well. But looking back, I think the real defeater of her fear was her faith. She was afraid, but she did it anyway. She knew God was with us, and if she kept working, He would save us.

I peered through the fog-filled windshield, canvassing the remote area. The defroster was on high, and the wipers flew at quick speeds, providing a clearer view of Mom. She bore the resemblance of a woman with superhuman strength—agitated, pacing from one end of the front end to the other, and constantly surveying our surroundings. In a frenzy, she used her muscle, might, and all of her five-foot-eight, 150-pound frame to try to free us. At 42 years old, melting snow constantly dripping down her face—Mom was in a quandary.

About 50 minutes or an hour after I skidded off the road and landed us in a whiteout mess, I saw mom's desperation. I saw her brute strength. I saw a faith I couldn't fully understand. But I was afraid. Her efforts seemed futile. All of her hard work scraped away the snow, revealing the ice below, producing a slick surface and less traction for our tires to stick.

I squirmed—scared she was going to freeze out there. Every time Mom jumped into the car to warm up for a minute or two, ice water flowed from her hair, down to her face and landed in her lap. She rubbed icy, swollen red fingers together, forcing them between her thighs and the car's heating vents.

"Momma, it's so cold. You're going to freeze to death, Momma. Please stay in the car," I begged.

I had been driving to give Mom a break from our trip to a St. Louis hospital. It had been one of our frequent 15-hour day hospital trips to take my sister, Melissa, to get special treatments for her Muscular Dystrophy. The drive was only two-and-a-half hours from our home in Wilson City, Missouri, but it always meant a marathon day of getting up at 5:00 a.m., leaving our house by 6:00 a.m. to arrive in St. Louis nearly three hours later. Missy would go through a battery of tests and doctor visits for hours of treatment.

That particular night, we were getting a home a little later than normal. It was probably 9:00 or 10:00 p.m. A freshman in college, I was a good driver, so I asked Mom if I could help with the drive home. I could tell she was exhausted. She quickly said yes, which confirmed my suspicion she was in no shape to drive.

I had no problems on the snowy Highway 55 South with the freeway plowed and salted. When I took the Benton/Dielhstadt exit onto the country road, it was a different story. The two-lane road filled with snow, and conditions seemed to be getting worse. Momma asked if I was afraid and if she should take over.

"I'm okay, Momma. I'm not afraid."

"Take it slow. There ain't no salt on these roads, and I wonder when the plows will get to them."

I was all too familiar with a sharp curve on the dimly lit road. I had taken it many times before, so I slowed down to about 30 right before taking it, but to my surprise, the car started sliding. In a panic, I jerked the wheel, and within seconds, I had spun our vehicle off the road into a snowbank. The car tilted downward slightly, stuck deep in ice, snow and slush.

"Please help me Lawd, help me and my children." Momma looked around the car. "Shit, Shit, Shit!" (Christians do cuss even though they may ask God for forgiveness immediately afterward.)

"Romona, how in the hell did you run off the road?"

"I don't know, Momma, I think I took the curve too fast, and when I hit my brakes, it just started spinning and sliding." I tried to explain, rubbing my hands together in a praying motion.

I began to cry, silently asking God to help us as well.

Melissa, nine years my junior, peered from the back seat of the car. Her limited muscle strength would not allow her to help us in any way. At the time, she spent most of her time in a wheelchair, aided by a walker. The sudden onset and discovery of the disease affected her walking and essential basic skills. She struggled with bathing herself, combing her hair, swallowing and even her sight at times. One look at her face told me she was frightened.

All of a sudden, a twinkle popped up in Mom's eye, and excitement burst from her. "Romona, pop the trunk again. I jus' remembered somethin'."

With a desperate and delirious look on her face, Mom frantically marched back to the trunk of our car. I heard her tossing stuff around like a madwoman, not knowing what she searched for.

I rolled down the window. "Momma, what are you doing?" I screamed loud enough so she could hear me. She didn't answer.

"Momma," I yelled again, "what are you doing? You're going to get sick out there. Momma!"

"Just hang on, Romona. I think I found somethin' that's gonna help." Mom slammed the truck. "Damnit, I forgot I had these bags."

Neatly tucked in front of the old plastic bags were some brown croaker-sacks we used to put our fresh garden-grown sweet potatoes in when we transported them to share with neighbors. They were burlap bags, made of course, abrasive material, and could hold several pounds of potatoes. The ones she had were about three- or four-feet wide by five feet in length. The heavy fabric itched when it made contact with your skin, but it just might provide the traction Mom needed to rescue us.

She placed the abrasive bags under the back tires on top of the ice, hoping that would do the trick. She also tried to dislodge some of the white stuff around the wheels. She placed two blocks of wood she managed to dig from underneath four to six inches of snow, which the car's headlights revealed. She pressed them snug in front of the two front tires to prevent the car from rolling forward.

Again, she instructed me to put the transmission in reverse and floor it as she jumped in front of the car, pushing backward with every bone in her body.

I did what she said, but my emotions overwhelmed me. I feared we'd never get out, and it was my fault we were stuck. I continued to obey her commands as tears streamed down my face.

Mom, still in front of the car gazing at me and yelled, stop cryin', keep the wheels straight, and keep flooring the accelerator in reverse. I was afraid I would flood the engine because I had seen Mom do it a few times before when our worn Chevrolet wouldn't start, and she desperately needed the decades-old vehicle to get her to work.

The bald tires continued to produce grinding and squealing noises the more I applied my foot on the accelerator. The seconds felt like minutes. My mind was racing. Mom pushed the front bumper with seemingly herculean strength, yelling for me to floor it again. Each time the car rocked violently back-and-forth, I felt it would go over the planks and crush my mom—especially if she slipped and fell. I wiped away my tears and floored it again.

That Chevy's tires must have liked its meeting with the croaker-sacks. As my grip tightened around the steering wheel, and the car popped and fired on all cylinders, I suddenly felt traction. It shot backward onto the road, and we were free.

Back on the road, I paused for Mom to get in the car. She motioned for me to slide into the passenger seat, immediately boosting the heat and rubbing her hands together repeatedly. They had become raw and reddish in color. Her coat and hair drenched, she had forced her coat's collar inside out to provide some warmth to her neck and chin.

She looked haggard, but there were no signs of the physical pain Mom must have endured. She calmly and carefully steered that Chevy through the snow, not uttering a word—just laser-focused on the road. Melissa was tucked in the backseat, not saying a word, and I had started to cry again.

"I'm sorry, Momma."

"Stop that cry'n. We're OK. You just panicked when you hit the curb too fast. Next time, turn your wheel into the slide and not away from it. Romona, what you focus yo mind on, you gonna be sensitive to it. You gotta be strong. You cry too much. Drop it. Forget about it. We're okay. I ain't mad at you." A look of resolve enveloped her face.

I kept watching her as she drove down the narrow, dimly lit road, never uttering another word about what we had just endured. In that moment, at 18 years old, I hoped I would inherit her tenacious power, courage, and faith to face adversity.

I had worked up a hunger after our late-night scare. I could smell the food in the brown paper bag next to my feet. Mom always packed two sandwiches a piece for our long day trip to the hospital. We could never afford the assortment of hospital cafeteria delights or the McDonalds we coveted along Interstate 55, but she always made certain we had something to eat. Normally, Melissa and I would salivate during the trip, dreaming and craving a chance to chomp on Big Macs like we'd hear some of the other kids rave about in school. Not on that day, though. As I eased the bag up to my lap under the night's sky, it was still light enough I could smell and see specks of grease staining the bag. The oil spots indicated the mayonnaise on my favorite, a fried ham sandwich, seeped through the paper towel wrapping and soiled the bag.

It was much-needed comfort food on a night that provided little comfort. The white lightbread had adhered to the mayo, cold and hardened, not its usual soft, fluffy texture—proof our dinnertime meal had been delayed. I reached back over the passenger seat to hand Melissa her sandwich and offered to unwrap Mom's, but she wasn't hungry. She said she wanted to keep her eyes on the road.

I felt around in the bag to find the bottle opener Mom always packed to pop the top off our six-ounce Coca-Cola® bottle. I can still remember how satisfying the pairing of that soda and sandwich tasted. I loved biting into my ham and then chasing it with the Coke. That quick burst of burn the soda produced in the back of my throat still ignites so many of my childhood memories.

Looking back, that moment taught me so much about the unrelenting strength of a woman. Like her, many of you have risen to heroine status in times of trouble—trouble on your jobs, in your marriage, with your kids, health scares, just stuff life throws at you. Sometimes, you don't realize how tough you are when you face roadblocks of pain and misery.

Like my mom, you feel unsafe, and your back is against the wall. You're overwhelmed with crippling thoughts that you can't climb out of your situation. That is when you call on Jesus and then come out fighting the enemy, with God's strength, to save yourself.

What I've Learned...
Faith in the Face of Tough Times

Without a doubt, I know my mom was filled with faith that night on that dark and desolate road. As her mind raced, trying to figure out how to save us, her voice remained strong, resolved, like she knew something my sister and I didn't. Throughout my childhood, she used the words faith and grateful hundreds of times.

"What if some did not have faith? Will their lack of faith nullify God's faithfulness?" (Romans 3:3 BSB)

Faith in the face of fear pleases God. He loves obedience. Faith gets His attention. Faith will allow the unbearable somehow to become bearable.

When dealt a cruel hand, scripture, faith, and prayer filled my arsenals. They were the fuel that fed me during extremely painful and unfair times.

"Now faith is being sure of what you hope for and certain of what you do not see." (Hebrews 11:1 NIV)

I could never see that just around the corner, God was about to provide a downpour of favor in my life. He was about to pour me out a blessing that I would not have room enough to receive it. God is the great equalizer when life is unfair.

Even when I've been in the midst of a storm in my life, being haunted by disturbing thoughts of failure, I would still start my morning smiling, thanking God. Smiling is an easy way to change the whole tone of your day. I know, forming creases in your mouth to produce a smile during troubles sounds silly to some, but for those who know the power of God, you know there are no limits to His power.

You can't please God without faith. Many of us claim to have deep abiding faith. The problem lies in the fact there are different degrees of faith. There is a huge difference between weak and strong believers.

"We who are strong ought to bear with the failings of the weak and not to please ourselves." (Romans 15:1 NIV)

Some of us who are stronger in our faith should step in and encourage those who are going through difficult times. I learned long ago, "strength is for service, not status." That is why I now share my unmovable faith with those who need it.

It is easy to have faith when God intervenes quickly and rescues us from our pain. Our faith weakens when we're left to endure the storm for months or years. That is when we need strong believers who can see clearly without a doubt, God has not forgotten you. They need to know, like Peter on the water, they should look more steadily at Jesus, and less at the waves and the wind.

I've prayed with female sisters of all races, crippled by loss and loneliness—afraid of what tomorrow might bring, but they remained faithful to God. Some told stories of celebrating a life of triumph and joy, only to be emotionally bruised by break-ups or divorce, but they kept the faith. Others shared stories of going from perfect health and strength—both mental and physical— to facing a devastating illness, but they remained faithful. Many told tales of being caught in the trapdoor of depression and anxiety with seemingly no way out, but they continued to believe in the Word and God's healing powers.

I have experienced some of the most amazing things in my life just when I felt it was time to give up. In 2011, I was about to leave my beloved Cleveland for a television job out of town. I wrestled with paralyzing thoughts of being unemployed if I didn't leave. Again and again, I prayed and called on God. He didn't answer. I couldn't hear His voice, so I thought it was over. I believed the voices that told me it was time to move on. Just when I was about to leave, my agent called. I would be signing a multi-year deal to remain in town. Voices of fear had won out over my faith. I was about to go ahead of Him. God will test your patience, your faith, and you are capable of passing the test.

I don't have the audacity to try to tell you how to live your life, what your hang-ups or truths are. We may all suffer some of the same issues, but we're uniquely and intricately made by God, so we might handle problems differently in our time and in a way that suits us.

Many of us will hold God's hands in the face of danger and fear. While some of us are natural worrywarts, we tell ourselves we can't do this, I don't have that. But when you have fierce faith and harness God's words, you can turn that panic into prayer, asking Him to save you. *Know that your storm is your story, and faith in the Lord Jesus is the only sure medicine for your troubled heart.*

I could actually see problems in my life start to disappear when I filled my faith prescription and began to believe more thoroughly, trust more entirely, and lean on Him more completely.

Chapter 9

NEEDING—AND BEING—A FEARLESS FRIEND

Life's adversity has a way of throwing us into a tailspin—keeping us focused on problems, not what God promises. That's when it helps to have some of those surprisingly remarkable people—friends who possess unbelievable, unshakeable faith and will never desert you when you need them. Their hearts are pure, their motives are clear, and they're God's way of taking care of us on our journey.

The kind of friend who's always got your back, no matter what. She will travel down the road of misery with you through breakups, job loss or illness—all the while providing the super support you need until you bounce back. Even if you're the person causing all the craziness and chaos, she will likely be there when you're done being the messiest of messy.

I had that kind of friend during my freshman year in college. Jeanette was a big girl with a big personality, one that lit up a room on campus. She flaunted a statuesque presence—what some people might call thick. At five-ten-and-a-half, a little north of 200 pounds, chocolate skin and dark brown eyes with natural semi-curly course hair, she was one of my friends and a sight to behold. Her big and bold presence might be intimidating to some, but when she flashed her beautiful smile, it disarmed you. Like me, she was from the backcountry, rural southeast, Missouri. She grew up an hour or so from where I did. We hit it off well because she was a country girl too—she understood the feeling of going without and not having experienced the finer things in life. She had such a magnetic personality, and like me, a real thirst to succeed in the world.

The night of my birthday, we went to a party off-campus. It felt like we stayed on the dance floor all night. As the DJ played 70's and 80's hit after hit, we high-fived one another and celebrated my nineteenth birthday. Suddenly, I started to feel a little dizzy and needed to go back to my seat. My dance partner, also a classmate, walked me back to my table. I wasn't sure if it was the cheap concoction of the Mad Dog drink Jeanette and I smuggled into the club. We couldn't afford much else. No one ever carded us. It might have been that our height made us look legal. Jeanette was still dancing the night away, motioning at me every once in a while with her hands in the air. I took another sip of my other drink, thinking my stomach did not agree with the wine.

Soon after, a popular and handsome fraternity member, who had bought me a second drink, came over and asked if I was okay. I looked up and began to answer him, but his face was a little blurry. I don't know if I got any words out. I don't remember much about the night from that moment, except what Jeanette told me the next day.

She saw me being led out of the club by the fraternity guy, and when she shouted, "Romona, where are you going?" I didn't even look at her.

The guy gave her a stern, angry look and yelled back over the loud music, "She's going with me!"

Jeanette, thank goodness, remembered our girl pact. We never leave one another alone in a bar. Our friendship and safety always came first. She quickly grabbed my arm. My pupils looked dilated. It was as if I was looking right through her. Jeanette knew something was wrong because I'd never been a heavy drinker—one or two max while partying.

She recalled trying to pull me away from the guy, but he resisted and snatched my arm, shouting, "She wants to go with me!"

Jeanette asked me if that was true, and I didn't or couldn't answer.

Somehow, with her fiercely loyal determination and gut instinct that something was very wrong, Jeanette got me away from that guy.

I remember waking up in my dorm room bed the next morning with a terrible headache and stomachache. After talking with some of the more experienced party girls on campus, Jeanette and I believed I must have been slipped a mickey. I didn't even know what that was. I was astounded when they told me a certain kind of man would put the drug in a girl's drink to paralyze her body and mind for a while. It had to have been what happened to me. I had a vague memory of Jeanette saying something to me, and this guy shouting at her, but I didn't have the ability to speak. Everything seemed to move in slow motion.

We learned a valuable lesson that night. "Never, ever leave your drink unattended!"

I also learned Jeanette was "that kind of girl"—that fearless friend who's got your back. The kind of friend God sends to guide and protect you. The kind of friend that is nothing short of a gift from God.

Soon after, I had a chance to prove if I was that kind of friend too. I stumbled a bit, but my devotion to my friend was no match for the kind of power plays some men pull.

A few weeks later, while Jeanette and I were eating lunch in the cafeteria, she noticed one of the star football players, Raymond, staring at me. We started to giggle like teenagers—because we were. I always thought he was so handsome. He was about 6-foot, 2-inches, nearly 200 pounds, with an incredible, muscular build. His skin was silky smooth like chocolate pudding, no acne in sight. When he walked, it was as if time stood still, and all the girls watched.

That day, he was walking toward me.

Jeanette grabbed my hand with her eyes fixated on Raymond and whispered, "Romona, he's coming over here!"

Before I could even turn to look, he was at our table and asked if he could talk to me for a minute.

I said, sure, I'd meet him outside in a minute when I was finished with my lunch.

After he walked away, I started to breathe again—I hadn't noticed I stopped for a few seconds!

Jeanette and I both wanted to scream, but we realized people were watching and we'd have to act like this was no big deal. She held my hand so tight and started to pinch me with excitement.

"Do you realize who just said they want to talk to you?" she whispered.

"Of course," I said, trying to hold back my grin.

"How can you be so calm?"

"He just wants to talk to me, and maybe it's not to ask me out." I tried not to get my hopes up.

"Please. The way he just looked at you? Oh yeah, he's gonna ask you out." Enthusiasm raised her voice. "So what are you waiting for, girl? Go see what he wants." She let go of my hand.

Nervous and somewhat uncomfortable with attention from one of the school's star athletes, I walked outside. Raymond was waiting for me, staring at me. He seemed so comfortable and confident, and without hesitation, he got straight to the point.

"I've been checking you out, Romona, and I like what I see. You want to hang out sometime?"

I knew I should hesitate just a little bit, but he was one of the finest boys I ever saw. So, I quickly belted out, "Yes, I'd love to!" I couldn't suppress the grin spreading over my face.

"There's a dance this weekend at the student union on campus. You want to meet me there?" He already knew what my answer would be.

"I'd like that." I knew the sheepish grin on my face probably looked like a star-struck teenager.

"Great, I'll meet you there," he said quickly as if he had done this many times before.

"Okay, I'll see you then."

As I turned to walk away, Jeanette almost bumped right into me. "Girl, I was waiting around the corner for him to leave. Did he ask you out? Tell me. Did he ask you out?" She shouted and pulled on both my hands,

"Yes, he did. We're going to meet at the student union party."

"I told you he liked you," she said, smiling. "You've got to tell me all the details."

Raymond and I met at the party and had a great time talking and dancing. It was the start of a short romance.

A few weeks after the dance, we hung out, and as he turned to walk away from me, he looked back quickly over his shoulder and said, "You know, Romona, one more thing before you go."

"Yes?" I turned to him, smiling, so pleased with how handsome he looked.

"Lose the big fat, ugly friend. She doesn't look good hanging with you." He never missed a beat, the statement flowing with total ease.

My heart stopped. I was shell-shocked. I suddenly felt out of breath. I couldn't believe what I had just heard. How could he say something so hurtful and mean about my friend? Completely stunned, I couldn't even utter a word back to him to defend her! I simply kept walking.

Jeanette never knew why I stopped seeing Raymond that night. I didn't even reveal it to him after my repeated objections to his advances.

"So what's up with you? Why won't you go out with me again?" he asked a short time later.

"I'm really not interested in dating anyone right now, Raymond," We never spoke of his awful remark about my girlfriend, but I knew I could never be with someone who could be so cruel.

Looking back, I wish I had the strength and confidence I now possess. I would have gotten right up in his face and told him never to say something so cruel about my friend—that she was beautiful, body and soul, the most important of which he was apparently lacking!

I was afraid back then, afraid of confrontation, fearful of challenging people who are cruel. My answer was to walk away rather than be assertive. But now I know God wanted me to be the friend who spoke up. One that would use the power of my voice rather than just walk away. I chose to be a loyal friend to Jeanette, but I could've been even more.

What I've Learned… Sisterhood

Are you that brave girlfriend who can look past the idea of beauty, the perfection the world says you must achieve? The girl who's not afraid of rejection and will stand-up for a friend who needs you to be stronger than she feels in the moment? Are you the woman who's not afraid to challenge the status quo? The person who says I can achieve whatever I set my mind to and work for it? Can you be a special light for those who live in the darkness of sorrow because life may not have been kind? But most of all can you be the woman God created you to be—Courageous, Kind, Gritty, yet Passionate and Purposeful.

Are you the confident sister who also empowers other women along the way and knows her success is not her own? A true friend willing to hold her hand and pray when the road gets scarier and harder. That precious friend who stands by her in moments of hardship and turmoil. She wipes away tears and fears during illness. A friend who accepts flaws and never walks away. Are you that faith-filled fearless friend who will fight when no one else will? That rare, special person God sends to make life on this earth better.

These friends are a gift from God, because only through God's strength and love and God's understanding of what's important in life can we set ourselves aside to be there—bold, beautiful, brave, no matter what—for our friends, without worrying what others think of us. When you're committed to God and see life through his eyes, you can be that friend—the friend each of us needs.

Chapter 10

Discerning God's Voice

I heard God's calling in December 2016. I had been offered a multiyear contract renewal to stay on as primary anchor at WOIO-TV in Cleveland. I didn't have to mull over the decision. It had already been made for me. The voice of God had spoken. It wasn't the kind of earthly, loud tone you hear with your ears—it was more a marathon of whispers I would hear sometimes morning, noon, and night. It nagged me at night, clouded my thoughts during the day—an unrelenting voice that I could no longer ignore.

It was time to leave my job at WOIO-TV and chart a new season—focusing on spreading hope, faith, unity and purpose through my books. It was what I had grown to love—speaking in front of live audiences, testifying about God's goodness.

Some of my favorite talks were about the negative voices I heard growing up in poverty. How you're made to feel inadequate, insecure, how poverty is all you'll ever know because of your zip code and who your parents are not, and how I had to find strength through the Word of God to fight back against the ugly mutters that plagued my thoughts.

My story started to grow and catch fire when audiences became receptive to my messages of how I put a stop to voices that told me I wasn't good enough. They whispered

I would never become a journalist like my idol, the legendary evening news anchor, Walter Cronkite, because I was poor, black, I spoke broken English, and I went to a small "black college." I couldn't measure up to kids from Ivy League schools who mostly came from prominent or middle-class families. The lies danced in my head for decades. My speeches of weeding out worry with worship resonated with listeners who shared they too had been listening to the mentally debilitating lies Satan told about themselves—lies saying you're worthless, you're fat, you'll never be successful, nobody loves you and no-one ever will.

The more I spoke about my life and listened to the experiences of others, the surer I became that Satan will sabotage your life, your marriage, ruin your children, and distance you from your friends and family. He does it by feeding on your feelings of hopelessness. He searches for those weaknesses in your armor and exploits them.

Even though I was immersed in joy, spreading my faith as any good reporter would, I questioned the voice I was hearing.

"Are you sure, God? Television is all I've ever known."

The voice responded even louder. "Yes."

But I still questioned, "Is this the will of God, or is it my own voice, my own wish of ending my career and moving in a new direction? I struggled with the decision.

As I considered what was ahead, I looked back over my career. I had the honor and privilege of telling incredible stories over a 30-year career in Cleveland. As an eight-time Emmy award-winning anchor, and recipient of the Edward R Murrow Award with my station, I had won every prestigious award I sought and ones I didn't. I traveled across the country, covering and interviewing presidents and dignitaries. I rubbed elbows with some of the most influential people in the country and served my city well. I worked with some incredible journalists and friends who wanted to do great work, but I wasn't entirely fulfilled. I only did what felt comfortable, what was familiar. But it was not enough. God kept calling me to do more.

I decided to opt for a two-year deal that would run through January of 2019.

In preparation for this life change, I started to delve deep into the Word. My daily morning scriptures took on an even greater meaning. The small and sometimes loud voice came to me in my quiet moments. The directive to transition grew louder each month, a tugging at my heart that God was calling me to move in a new direction.

On New Year's Day 2018, I asked God, as I do every January 1, "What is it you would have me do this year?"

The answer did not come as a shock to me, but some of those closest to me wondered if I was making the biggest mistake of my career. God told me it was time to move on after I finished my contract.

In December 2018, I said goodbye to my television career. I'd be lying if I said there was no last-minute trepidation about the end. I'm human, and when you start listening to voices—those that claim you're committing career suicide, no one will care about you, buy your books or will not want to hear you speak because you're no longer relevant and you will fade in the background becoming yesterday's news—you start to second-guess your decision.

Anxiety and worry can creep in if you don't keep your focus on the Lord. That's when you have to dig deep. You have to take control of your thoughts, weed out the distortion, and tell yourself you are making the right decision. If I truly believed God was redirecting me, moving me into a new season of my life, I had to have faith things were going to work out. When I couldn't see the road ahead, I knew I needed to do it anyway—even when my faith started to waver.

I knew you don't make a lot of money selling books, so my monthly intake would be minuscule compared to my television salary. I started praising God and thanking my mom, who taught me to save for a raining day. I was finally in a position to do what I wanted to do when I wanted to do it and not answer to anyone but my Lord and Savior. That's a big deal for a girl who grew up in poverty.

My husband and I had drawn a picture in our minds, and on paper, how we would live out our new season. It would include a lot of service, several speeches, and lots of travel as I started dwindling down that 15-item bucket list. We'd continue Romona's Kids, honoring children working hard to succeed. We'd spend more time with friends and family and really get closer to our faith. I didn't have to worry if God would furnish the increase—He already had throughout my life.

"For God is the one who provides seed for the farmer and then bread to eat. In the same way, he will provide and increase your resources and then produce a great harvest of generosity in you." (2 Corinthians 9:10 NIV)

So even when the negative voice would creep in, that quiet, and sometimes-loud voice was telling me God will reward you for your faithfulness. He will provide the resources you need to do His work.

I noticed when I second-guessed my decision, it was always about my comfort, safety, and security, eliminating all risks. However, being comfortable can steal all of the passion and joy in your life. Maybe that's why I started to feel somewhat empty in my job for the first time in my life like I wasn't doing enough—it wasn't enough. I was not having a big enough impact on people's lives.

I knew that scripture says without faith, it's impossible to please God. So, I continued to live in faith. I had to allow God to barricade the road that was no longer the right way, and I had to follow on the new road he was leading me down.

During my journey, I found two kinds of voices that tried to sabotage me—voices that have sabotaged me in the past, voices that I've seen wreak havoc on other women's lives. Those voices are doubt and envy, and they speak a message counter to the message of God. They were the ones trying to lure me back down a road I knew was going nowhere.

Are you following the voice of doubt in your life? How many dreams die because your faith wanes, and you simply give up, deeming it too hard, tired of rejection, tired of failure. You find yourself doubting God, asking Him why He is taking you through this. Seeking how He's trying to shape and mold you by having this suffering in the journey be so tough while others seem to enjoy clear sunny days.

I wanted to be obedient, but I'm human. So, when close friends and family questioned my decision to leave my television career, and the unexpected death of my beloved mother shook me to my core, it was only natural for me to fall back into a state of fear and uncertainty.

But what if we could learn to trade our fear for the certainty that God's plans are good? Fear is the silent enemy that keeps us from reaching our God-given potential.

I fell back on a habit I'd practiced through life—one that I learned from my mother. When God's voice called me to do something, I did it.

Now, it's worth noting—as I mentioned, my husband and I didn't just throw caution to the wind and decide one day I'd leave my work, write books, and speak to the world. It took a lot of planning, soul searching and unstoppable faith.

When you are searching for affirmation about a problem or change, sometimes the answer can be found in scripture. God will speak to you through his Word. When I decided to make the life-changing moment, I had to lean on the scripture. I could not only trust the daily voices. My confirmation came one morning when I was filled with doubt. I sat up in bed as I tried to enjoy my morning cup of joe and started to ponder my future in complete silence. Suddenly, my phone pinged. It was my morning Bible Gateway scripture. I read the verse:

"The Lord is my light and my salvation-who shall I fear? The Lord is the stronghold of my life-of whom shall I be afraid?" (Psalms: 27:1 NIV)

I immediately thought, "With God on my side, I fear no one."

I felt the pull of God building up my confidence, reassuring me, gracing me with a clear understanding of the direction of my new chapter, one that included road signs to more service in my community. I could see He had already shown me through every corner and curve where my journey would lead me, giving me the tools I needed to go around roadblocks and sometimes-insurmountable hills, and how I've traveled to become successful.

I knew I was about to make a gigantic leap that would chart a new course in my future. At moments, I felt like I was in a holding pattern, waiting for the Lord to spell out his plan for me. But, finally, I was ready to fly. His timing was perfect.

I'm now a national award-winning author and motivational speaker and working with my husband—life is good. I speak to thousands of people about God's grace and mercy, and I'm having the time of my life. Once I embraced the direction the Lord was leading me, I could drown out the voices that told me to fear.

When you keep your eyes on God, you can overcome fear, no matter the obstacles you face.

The second voice I learned to recognize is envy—the voice driven by people who want what I have. Both voices put you at odds with others, separating you from the people God puts in your life, and if you give in to them, they contradict and drown out God's voice.

April 11, 2011, was one of the happiest days of my life, especially as a journalist. I had been granted an exclusive one-on-one interview with former President Barack Obama at the White House. I describe the moment in *A Dirt Road to Somewhere*. Such an interview represents a huge feat that's nearly impossible for a local anchor or reporter. Snagging a sit down with the leader of the free world can make your career—a coveted assignment any reporter worth their salt will attempt to get. I recall hearing the reaction of someone seeking the same interview, rejected by the White House. They suggested I was granted the prized invite because I was black, and so was the president. Even with eight Emmys for excellence in journalism, an Edward R Murrow award and many more, I was reduced to the color of my skin. That person's envy threatened to make me feel small in one of my proudest, yet most humbling moments.

Another time, when I won two of my Emmy awards in one night, someone who didn't win jokingly said to another colleague, "The judging must have been flawed that night."

How do you handle hurtful voices of jealousy and resentment? How do you push past the negativity and not allow it room to park in your brain? In my humanity, I admit it had a sting to it. But you have to recognize that voice for what it is. And sometimes you have to recognize when those voices come from your own mouth, voicing the envy you feel toward others.

The devil will come to you wearing sheep's clothing. He will use any means necessary to throw you off your path. He wants to keep you stuck right where you are, suffering and feeling alone. He salivates when you feel discouraged, unaccepted and unloved. What you're unwilling to walk away from is where you will get stuck.

Don't allow people to drag you down, people who convince you to settle where you are even if you're unhappy. Life is too short. You have the power to ignore the naysayers and rule your life, setting limits when needed and taking risks when necessary. When you align with your true self, people take notice. They see the confidence, the beauty inside you. Release the lies. You are the gatekeeper of your life and the decision of how to live it.

During my life, and during my career transition, I had many gut-wrenching conversations with myself. Who I am, who I want to be and more importantly, who God wants me to be. At times, I had to cast Satan out, verbally saying to him, "Devil be gone, you are not going to put thoughts of envy and distrust in my mind. You will not create havoc in my life or me."

When doubt and envy threaten your future, use faith to fight back against the ugliness that will enter into your space. You have to get God involved. He will meet you where you are as He prepares you for where He wants you to be. He has the power to defeat every lie, every enemy, and He'll never leave your side.

Some of us stay trapped in a situation even after God has given us the key and a way out. Does the voice of fear prevent us from taking the steps to freedom? Do we not believe we deserve better? It's the enemy's job to convince you to stay in prison. Only you can unlock the chains on guilt and shame you've been lugging around. You have been shackled by fear for so long you just accept it as normal. You are free to speak your truth and live a better life. We tell ourselves we're not strong enough, but that's because we repeat the false narrative we've been told most of our lives.

When you feel like you're not enough, remember God is. He's got your back.

"Then your light will break forth like the dawn, and your healing will quickly appear; then your righteousness will go before you, and the glory of the Lord will be your rear guard." (Isiah 58:8 NIV)

The glory of God will continue to pave your way. He will break the chains of your suffering and all the evil murmurs.

You can have your mind renewed and retrained through the Word of God.

What I've Learned... Becoming Confident in your Own Voice

Know who controls your thoughts about you. Is it the enemy? He will use your own mind and voice to plant doubt and ugliness about yourself. Let's face it, we choose to believe the negative thoughts others or we say about us. For some, these are lies you told yourself for years, and they stuck, so you started believing them.

God will send a clear message of who you are. He will reinforce your worth as a woman, a wife, a mother, a sister or a friend.

The world has a way of stealing your confidence—telling you you're not good enough, smart enough, pretty enough. You're not capable or courageous enough to bounce back from rejection and failure and step into your purpose. As much as you try to ignore the outside noise, words have value, and the tongue can rip you apart, so you start to second-guess yourself.

I now worry more about how I feel and less about what people might think about me. I have set new boundaries, and I've let go of my need to please, perform, and be perfect.

I had to silence those negative voices and preload my brain with positive thoughts, keeping some in reserve for whenever I need them.

I choose to believe what God says about me. He created you, and He knows you have something to offer to the world. You just have to find what that is. We all have the capacity to contribute in big and small ways.

But when you lack confidence in your abilities, it can leave you feeling inadequate, unsure if you have something to offer to society.

I read that 86 percent of people go to job sites they hate. Even though God was providing a way for me to transition out of television, I had to have enough confidence and trust in Him to know I had outgrown that job. If you can't MoveOn, when it's not right, life will MoveOn and leave you behind. Had I not been fired all those years ago in South Carolina, I never would have realized my dream. It was during those dark times I discovered who and what I was made of. I was able to ask myself, "What am I supposed to be doing with my life?" If you can't say what I'm doing right now, then you know you're not living your purpose. When we have problems, something earth-shattering in our life, we run to God only to discover God sent the storm. He wants to grow your faith, your confidence in Him.

I think life comes down to the choices we make and how we choose to deal with stuff—whatever is thrown our way—good and evil. When you become mature in your faith, you will develop the mental and moral courage and strength to stand up in the face of adversity and withstand the hit. Individual good qualities make you uniquely you. You should never compromise your religious beliefs to satisfy others.

Get clear on what you want, and develop confidence in yourself. If you feel stuck, consider whether you're truly tapping into the talents God gave you and whether you're seeking to grow.

Proverbs 22:29 says, "Do you see someone skilled in their work?" Learn from people who are skilled at things you aspire to. Those people are constantly working to get better at their craft, learning new things. Don't let where you are currently be an excuse not to grow. Don't be a complainer, but a problem solver. If you don't like something, always try to have a solution.

Throughout my life, I've always had a personal growth plan, yet always remained open to allow God to lead me. Growth is not automatic. It takes work. Are you reading books, listening to Podcasts, taking any online courses, going to Bible study, to seminars, interested in a hobby? Do you have any mentors? Don't just coast through life. You have a treasure on the inside of you. There are skills and talents put in you by the creator.

You have to prepare yourself for what you want and be ready when God delivers. Learn about the future you want, sharpen up now. Don't wait, thinking, after I get that big break, then maybe I'll take those courses. No, prepare for what you want. When God sees you are prepared, He will reward you.

The enemy would love to distract you, keep you away from your destiny, and stop you from moving forward or moving on. Don't let fear and lack of confidence in your abilities hold you back from creating a better life for yourself. Own who you are—what you like, what you don't like, what you want to change—and develop a plan to make the changes.

Chapter 11

Silencing the Enemy

"Romona was fired! Don't believe she wanted to leave Channel 19. She was fired." The troll posted on my personal fan page.

It was September 2018, when I posted a heartfelt goodbye and statement I had given to our local paper, sharing with viewers and my social media friends why after thirty-one years in Cleveland television, it was time for me to start my new season. I received countless posts from well-wishers, an outpouring that touched me in ways I will forever be grateful for. But even with the hundreds of positive messages, two women, who didn't know me and knew nothing about my personal business or career, decided to start a negative thread, disputing my account of why I was leaving television.

Another troll posted, "She isn't really nice."

"I was in a dressing room at a department store and heard her yelling at a saleswoman who wasn't bringing her clothes fast enough!"

I will admit, at first, I was shocked by the accusation and suffered a short bout of anxiety—worried about what others who didn't know me and saw the post might think. Would they believe I would be so rude to anyone, ever?

She went on to claim other women witnessed my outbursts, and the saleswoman was visibly shaken. But, anxiety will kill your spirit. When you suffocate your thoughts, fearing things that don't matter, you don't allow your faith room to breathe. You become vulnerable to the voice of the enemy—giving them the power to steal your joy.

I wondered how someone could make up a lie about me and spread it for all to see. Anyone who knows me at least knows I'm not a yeller and then I remembered what Oprah Winfrey said. "Align your personality with your purpose, and no one can touch you." Those words rang true with me.

Now, at one time in my life, the faint-faith Romona would click on their profiles, take the bait and respond to the noise. But my life is full. I can't be deterred. God has set me on a path to inspire and encourage our youth and empower women who feel powerless.

I suspect those women are probably living a life of unhappiness, hoping to disrupt my path with lies and taunts. I get it now. When people are punched and knocked down, they want to punch back at the first thing they see, and if it happens to be a woman who appears to have it all then that's the target. *I have learned over the years that how you live your life reflects what you send out to the world*. So, I chose to foster love and kindness.

The avalanche of images we see on social media can make us feel like we don't measure up to the great lives our peers seemingly have. Sometimes, we lash out at others because we are lacking in our lives.

But when you're able to find "your" worthiness and no longer feel like you have to live up to the idea of someone else's perceived success, it is powerful. You get good results when you let go of perceived perfection. You can come in last and still feel a sense of fulfillment and achievement. You didn't quit the race you finished. You can't say to yourself "nothing is gonna stand in your way" if you fall apart when someone challenges or rejects you.

Your identity is secure in God, but in order to fully live that way, you have to shut out the other voices that try to tell you who you are. These are the voices of the enemy, and they plague us from every direction.

When you are living your true self, trolls have no power over you. I was on a course to fulfill Gods calling in my life, and I was obedient in my walk. Satan doesn't like that, so he sends his distractions to try and block progress.

Some people are just mean and angry about their lot in life, but they do nothing to try and change things. Does that give them the right to lash out and spew ugliness about others? Of course not. But when you're living in a space that doesn't allow negativity to block your journey, you learn to ignore the noise, the messiness.

Don't carry around other people's baggage.

Develop new habits like wearing the armor of God to shield you from antagonistic voices, and grow a thicker skin, providing protection from the negative Nellies, so other people's opinions don't upset you. (Journalists have used this mental tool for years to clear the noise of people who disagree with our reporting.) Use that mental shut off valve. *Reprogram your brain to repel nonsense.* Block them out. Focus on what you believe to be right. You can't allow them to control you. If you let them push your buttons, they will visit you often and invade your space.

When you start talking badly about somebody on social media, you're downloading misery straight from the devil's den. You're streaming hateful rhetoric live, and it excites him. God will tell you good things about yourself, but the devil refutes the good and reinforces the bad—all of the insecurities you have. He replays the negative—you're too fat, you don't like your nose, mouth, butt or legs. You wish you were someone else—maybe like the Kardashians or other attractive women you see on social media.

The devil has designed a plan to penetrate your thoughts and make you feel less than. It's critical that he taps into your sins, your secrets, things you want to hide from the world. He will hold on to them and expose you when you least expect it. He wants your salvation, and he has several minions on social media doing his dirty work. When some people feel hurt, they want to lash out and make someone else feel pain. It's the oldest trick in the book by Satan—divide and conquer. They may be slaving away in a dead-end job and see someone else on social media posting pictures about their successful career. Someone shows images of her handsome husband and beautiful baby, and they have no one, so jealousy drives them to cut that person down somehow.

Even though we know what envy looks and feels like, we aren't robots, and our feelings are hurt, so we want to lash out and react to the negativity. But that's the enemy's way.

The enemy has not stood much of a chance in my life since I realized God has been protecting me from harm and providing me with a guiding light to help enlighten the lives of others.

And, there's something about entering your fifties. That milestone in your life produces more confidence. You're clearer about who you are as a woman, a wife, a sister and a friend. You know what you want personally and professionally. Even if you don't have complete clarity about what you should be doing, you've probably figured out how and where you're going. That said, it's never too late to change directions.

Social media can be a wonderful tool for sisterhood and empowerment. I have joined some spiritual and inspirational Facebook pages and chat frequently. Those conversations are uplifting and feed the soul. You can find a wealth of information and education concerning just about any issue you're dealing with, career and entrepreneurial sites that empower you. You are connected to people all over the world who can spark creative and innovative ideas inside that you didn't know existed. In addition to my motivational quotes on social media, I follow like-minded people who motivate and push me to be better.

Unfortunately, all the tweeting, posting and Insta-chats anonymously can be a breeding ground for jealousy, perfection, rejection. We compare ourselves to women and girls our age, and it makes us measure our self-worth. We don't have the type of clothes, flawless makeup, the perfect job or waistline, the perfect boyfriend. We become depressed. Depression will tell us the ugliest thoughts about ourselves. Instead, try looking at the beauty within you that's already there. Trust what "you" have to offer.

The enemy will set up shop in your mind 24/7. Stop seeking your life—whether it's what you wanted or not—through someone else's eyes.

The next time you're scrolling through social media posts, comparing your life to others listen to the right voices—the Holy Spirit will feed us positive things about ourselves. Satan will punch you with one negative thing after another until he latches on, tearing you down mentally piece by piece, and making you feel like you don't measure up to the images.

We're a vessel that needs maintenance. The enemy will use the mouths of others as a tool to hurt you. Only you can provide your psyche or soul with mental love and care. A psychologist can help you with deep-seated issues, but ultimately, you have to be willing to push past the fear and seek help if you need it. Many of us were raised to believe you don't seek professional help to deal with your problems. You just need to be strong and deal with stuff. I know now I could have avoided a lot of long-suffering in my life had I simply talked to a therapist about what I was going through.

Talking about fears and private matters in your life means you're comfortable and brave enough to wear your own skin—not feeling the need to appear perfect. Wear your battle scars and ignore the drama. If it costs your peace, it's too expensive.

Many of us suffer from comparisonitis instead of knowing we are uniquely made. There is no one else on the planet just like us. When you learn to be authentically you in any endeavor, it attracts a following. People can spot fakes, and they know when you're not truly interested in serving them.

Many women wear a facade, buying items with money they don't have to impress people on social media.

You sport the latest and greatest to impress your friends even though you're drowning in thousands of dollars in student-loan debt. You make up fake vacations, places you've Googled, to pretend you've been there so you can keep up and be seen as one of the cool people.

Regardless of the façade, God knows WHO YOU ARE—He created you. And you have to remember whose side you're on—God's—He will never leave you, and He wins every time.

"I will instruct you and teach you in the way you should go; I will counsel you and watch over you." (Psalms 32:8 NIV)

Stop relying only on GPS to get you where you want to go. Allow God to provide the direction and destination in your life—and the power to get you there. Then you have to follow His global positioning system. Your mind and social media will feed you lies about yourself, forcing you into bouts of mental anguish. Your joy comes in knowing God and believing He is watching over you. His Word says he will instruct you, teach you the way in which you should go. God has already mapped out your path. You just need to find what that is and follow it.

What I've Learned...
Hurt people, Hurt people

Life isn't a bunch of rainbows and unicorns. It can be tough. There is a divisive climate in this country. Many people are lashing out and spewing ugliness. They will talk bad about you. It will disappoint you and at times, threaten to damage you or your reputation. Problems can knock you off balance. But knowing who you are and where you're going and being willing to do the hard work to get there is half the battle. Let go of the evil distractions that remind you of whatever you fear—a health crisis, a break-up or financial struggles.

When the enemy attacks me, I ask God to increase my trust and faith in His willingness and ability to deliver me from my fear and anxiety. I stopped believing the hurtful and vile stuff some people dish out. It still hurts a bit, but it doesn't have that bite anymore. When you get into God's Word and ask him for a deeper meaning to your life, it's powerful to watch the revelation of His love, and how He moves in your life.

"An anxious heart weighs a man down, but a kind word cheers him up." (Proverbs 12:25)

Stop worrying about what people say or think about you. God knows your heart.

There will always be people unleashing a steady diet of complaints and negativity. If you don't agree with their views, they're mad. If you don't measure up to their expectations, they're upset. It's all trivial and not worth your precious time or good energy.

Turn your focus on the power of a God who can command negative bouts of fear to flee from your heart and mind.

Chapter 12

How Have You Been Called to Serve?

Sometimes it takes struggle to push us into our purpose. When things are comfortable we don't freshen up on new skills, we're not open to new friends or networking, we feel safe in our own bubble. But hardship has a way of forcing you out of those creature comforts.

God gives assignments to us—big and small—the kind where we sometimes ask ourselves, "Does He really want this for me? Is it God sending me into this uncharted territory? What if I fail the task?"

The uncertainty will eat away at us because many times, we're comfortable where we are, and we don't want to move or try something different. Even when God opens the door and waits for us to walk through it, we're hesitant.

We become consumed with thoughts of failure and what-ifs.

Even if you don't understand it, trust God. Stop fighting what He is not changing in your life. Stop being upset by what He's not removing.

God has never led me astray. He closed doors that weren't meant for me to walk through—averting huge mistakes. He literally gave me a push through open ones I was afraid to open. I shared the story in my memoir about my terrifying fear of covering the Ku Klux Klan in Charleston, South Carolina. As a young reporter given an assignment to cover a hostile Klan rally, I sat crouched in my news car with my photographer for a few minutes. Terrified to step out of the vehicle, I did it anyway. I was so uncomfortable with the assignment because they told me to get sound with the Klan's Grand Dragon who would be speaking.

God reminded me that day that my faith was my arsenal—the fuel that feeds me in a sometimes-cruel world and during encounters with bitter, hateful people. God protected me that day, and that story and others led to a highly successful journalism career that spanned more than 30 years.

Memories of my life and career run hot and cold in my mind. I've had to face insurmountable odds and been dealt what surely should have been knockout blows by vengeful souls. I believe it was important as a young journalist that I quickly see the good, bad and ugly side of humans and life in general. My calling then prepared me for the new season.

In May 2018, I planned to speak to a group of women in public housing.

Standing in a tight hallway, my colleague and I moved aside, allowing a woman space to continue walking, but overhearing my conversation piqued her interest.

"Why are you going into the hood? You're Romona Robinson. You should not be seen in the projects?" The stunning and unsolicited, obnoxious feedback came from this woman who stood within an earshot of me sharing with the colleague my excitement over speaking with these women about my life and career.

The woman continued. "You could be shot or killed."

I had to take a few deep breathes first to digest the disparaging remarks coming from her mouth.

"My dear brothers and sisters, take note of this: Everyone should be quick to listen, slow to speak and slow to become angry." (James 1:19 NIV)

I immediately thought of that scripture as I hesitated and gave my brain a chance to filter my thoughts before I spoke.

Unfortunately, my pause gave room for more insensitive remarks. "Will they even read your book?"

My eyes canvassed the full makeup of her youthful face. I tried to draw a picture in my mind of what might have caused a successful, intelligent and pretty, brown exterior to have such an ugly narrow view of people.

She recovered quickly. "Sorry, ladies. I didn't mean to interrupt your conversation. I just became a little concerned when I overheard you were going into a dangerous area."

"Thanks for your concern, but I'm not afraid," I shot back. "In fact, I'm excited. The woman who heads the program says her clients would be excited and receptive to my message of empowerment. She hopes my talk will further motivate them to work toward moving out of their situation."

My girlfriend remained silent the whole time, her facial expression flowing between a smile and a smirk, knowing if this conversation continued, the young lady was about to get a crash course of verbal whoop-ass in humility, compassion and respect from me—in a friendly tone, of course.

"Well, you're better than me. I would not feel comfortable going there."

I could tell from her sheltered perspective she wore a blindfold when it came to people she could not relate to. The mask she wore had jaded her thinking and trapped her mind, and sometimes, you just know when it would be a waste of time to argue a point with someone.

With some people, you have to let them live where they are. It is not your job to judge and bring them along. Looking back, I could have said to her that God is not as concerned about your comfort as He is your purpose.

He will let us become uncomfortable now so He can bless us later on. I somehow felt it would have fallen on deaf ears that day.

Until the storm comes blowing through your home, you can be judgmental and unwilling to open your mind and heart to people less fortunate. You have no interest in knowing their story, their struggle, or their pain.

I turned my attention away from the hater-raid being served up to focus on God's mission. I have remarkable compassion born from personal experience for people who are struggling to make lives better for themselves and their children.

The day of my appearance was a cold Cleveland winter day, but the temperature in the room was nice and toasty, and the personalities were equally as comforting.

A few of the 50 or so women, and some men, rushed to greet me as I walked through the door. Each one thanked me for coming. I've always found gratitude in how women especially feel comfortable instantly sharing their life's story with me—even after a few minutes of having met me. I have never been an instantaneous transparent person with a stranger—though many of these women treated me as if I were a sister or close family member. Their eyes filled with such joy laced with heartache as they reminisced about a life gone wrong. They told stories of a reality that had not been kind.

Many substantiated my thoughts that this was a visit where God felt I was needed and could do some good sharing my mom's incredible story of surviving mistakes, bad breaks and recovering from wrong turns in her life.

You could hear a pin drop as I shared how God rescued my mom from a life of abandonment, fears, and other challenges—how men who pedaled promises of love and support took advantage of her.

Like my mom, these women didn't wear filters to mask their pain. There were no blind spots in their memories about their harsh existence. They were candidly open about long-forgotten traumas that disrupted their lives and a myriad of problems that blocked their plans. One told me how loneliness after a breakup forced her to make poor choices. She seemed ashamed—yet needed to tell me how her new suitor robbed and left her penniless. She and her children, with nowhere to go, sought public housing.

She also talked about bouncing back from her missteps and the joy of enrolling in community college to provide a better life for her kids.

Another talked about the fear of being judged. She felt ashamed of allowing herself to fall victim to a lifetime of abuse. She sounded like a woman who bottled up her truth and couldn't wait to reveal her regrets for allowing drugs to take hold of her life, feeling inadequate and too paralyzed by fear to seek help.

I knew it would be a great day. After all, during my 30-year career, I had been in the projects many times featuring some of my beloved Romona's Kids who went on to become politicians, incredible athletes, judges and socially responsible adults.

The energy in the room was palpable. The ladies appeared to soak up my words, taking in my message.

I shared with them that God has the final say—failures are not permanent. Believe in the Lord, and He can change your life. He's just waiting to change you first.

I didn't have to wonder if I had an impact that day. My confirmation would come soon after that assignment. I was granted keynote speeches before two large organizations.

I had prayed for months to God about wanting to speak at huge women's conferences. It's where I thought I shined. But He led me off the beaten path to what He wanted from me. I was to go into the projects and speak to 50 women who needed to hear from me.

I thought of the young lady in the hallway that day. People who don't know you or get you will try to control who you are. Sometimes it is the enemy. He will use the voice of those near you to try and plant doubt and ugliness about other people.

I've always loved the quote by Mark Twain. "Keep away from people who try to belittle your ambitions. Small people always do that, but the really great make you feel that you, too, can become great."

I wonder if she might have put her foot in her mouth if she met former Starbucks CEO, Howard Schultz, that day in the hallway. He grew up in the projects of Brooklyn, New York. A self-made businessman rising from his humble beginnings, his family, at times, relied on a charitable organization for food. I was particularly interested in his description of the housing project he grew up in, saying it was "not designed to be a dead-end, but to jumpstart lives. He would later go on to create a business empire that revolutionized the way Americans consume coffee.

Business magnate Richard Branson talks about being dyslexic, filled with hopelessness, struggling in school, almost flunking out at thirteen years old. He was virtually shoved in the back of the class and forgotten about. But he recalls how he managed to overcome most of the difficulties by training himself to concentrate. He would eventually rise to prominence in the business world. He is shocked by the amount of time people waste dwelling on their past failures rather than directing that energy into a new project.

One of the reasons I love Oprah Winfrey is that she seems to live her truth. As a journalist, I was inherently drawn to her story and humble beginnings. She built a billion-dollar empire by staying true to who she was and not falling prey to what society said she should be. She has been so transparent, revealing her childhood truth, unafraid to be vulnerable about her abuse, fear and insecurities.

Mark Burnett, a television-producing giant of hit shows like Survivor, The Voice, Shark Tank, just to name a few, came to America more than 30 years ago with just two-hundred dollars in his pocket. He says a friend helped him find work as a nanny and housekeeper. He describes moving on to selling t-shirts—buying them for two dollars, selling them for eighteen, and saving his profits. He has been pretty vocal about the fact that strong faith and his prayer life has been a huge part of why he is successful, but he also credits good old-fashioned hard work and hustle. He had no education, little money, and he could have given up, but there is power in your struggle.

* * * *

There is also power in knowing how God wants you to serve. However, some people are not interested in what or where God is calling them to do work. They are comfortable living their everyday lives, raising their kids or taking care of themselves.

Some Christian women have shared with me that they have no idea of God's calling in their lives while others knew His purpose right away.

Does God place a calling on all of our lives? I believe so.

We just have to know how to listen, hear, and feel His presence. Sometimes it comes by way of an interruption. Remember LaToya in chapter one? Our conversation produced the clarity about the message and assurances I wanted to provide to the reader.

For you, it could be meeting someone whose godly walk mirrors how you'd like to live and challenges you to create your own new season. Maybe you've been longing to do something different or something more, but you're not sure where to start—watch for signs in likely and unlikely places. Some of you have been trying to change and live a good life and react to problems in a calmer more godly way, but you always fall short, and you feel empty deep down inside—listen to those quiet voices that whisper you can change.

I believe it's God calling you. He's drawing you close, saying, "I'm here when you're ready." It's up to you to answer the call.

"Behold I stand at the door and knock. If anyone hears My voice and opens the door, I will come in to him and dine with him, and he with me." (Revelation 3:20 NKJV)

When you feel that powerful pull like someone is pushing you in one direction even though you're trying to go in another, I've learned God is inviting you to let Him guide you, strengthen you and help you live and lead an incredible life.

For others, there might be a waiting period while He takes the time to grow you into His plan and your purpose. Some have told me they're waiting to stumble upon their true purpose, so they're still waiting. Others shared dreams of owning a business. But what if God has a different calling on your life? When do you know it's the right time to try something different? How do you know it's the proper time to pursue or let go of an idea? I found knowing comes in those quiet, still moments when I pray and listen to the voice of God. But you have to be willing to accept what you hear.

God set me on a fast-paced course. My God-filled calling continues to pour out of me as I write this book. I find myself so eager to pour into the reader what God has poured into my life; goodness, grace, favor, and a purposeful life!

I wanted to stress to readers that I know it is not easy to follow the path God maps out for you, especially if it's an uncomfortable one. But, He will not throw you out into your new purpose unless you're ready. Unbeknownst to me, He had been building my brand, my following, when I thought I was only building a television career. When I started my new venture, I was already a household name in Northeast Ohio, so my path was mapped out. Still, stepping out on faith and God's Word can be frightening. The voices of fear would visit often, but that's when God's angels show up.

"Do not forget to show hospitality to strangers, for by so doing, some people have shown hospitality to angels without knowing it." (Hebrews 13:2 NIV)

Total strangers had become my angels. On my social media pages, people offered to share posts about my book whenever I needed them. Some have shown up at my events and book signings, eager to help me in any way. I had other authors and business leaders voluntarily share my book launch in their newsletters. A local company put my upcoming memoir on a digital billboard. I know without a doubt, it was God's way of saying you are headed in the right direction, and I will send my shepherds to help.

What I've Learned… Do You

Listen to others, but don't lose your own voice. It's your power! And it's a powerful feeling when you truly get to know yourself.

You will meet people who will try to mold you into who they want you to be. People who say, if I were you, I would … Even after you have told them your God-led plan, they spell out their plan for you.

Trying to control, save, fix or change someone is exhausting. Sometimes, you have to let them live where they are. Allow them to grow at their own pace and not one you set for them. It's not healthy for you to keep pressuring someone to "Live the life" you have planned. That may not be their path. I want this book to create lasting change, getting to the root of why we feel a certain way—whether it's from toxic relationships, the environment in which you grew up, some hidden biases you have that you haven't dealt with. When you figure out the WHY, the HOW to change becomes clear.

We see people on social media making a lot of money hawking makeup, clothing, speaking, and we think, "I can do that. I'm gonna make a whole lot of money." You try to copy their passion. You haven't thought it out. You dive in headfirst, but you have no game plan or strategy or where you want to end up.

It is okay to emulate others as long as what they do is truly something you want to do. When you're in it just to make money and not serve others, it can be hard to maintain success that way. Every highly successful person will admit he or she helped people on the way up.

Stop chasing the latest, greatest, next big thing unless you're built for it. We don't all have the same tolerance for risk. I never was a high-risk taker. I fall somewhere in the middle. I know this about myself, so I can't be forced to do otherwise. We copy other people's ideas and dreams, and we're not ready. We haven't done the work, saved enough money and then wonder why we failed.

"God told me you were going to be the next Oprah!" a woman proclaimed to me once. "Thank you, miss, but I never wanted to be a talk-show host." God never told me National Talk Show Host would be part of my story. In order to please God, you may have to disappoint some people.

If people don't understand you, that's OK. If you lose some friends because you wouldn't let them control you, they weren't true friends anyway.

Your people-pleasing days must come to an end. Instead, you should please God with your good works as the Bible says.

God didn't tell me to leave television in two days and start to write books. There was a process. He allowed me to do what I loved for more than 30 years, grooming me for His calling all along—building my brand, name recognition, trust with my audience and allowing me room to do my homework to make sure I was ready.

If God's calling and timing in my life don't mirror yours, that's okay. Do you, in your time. Find what speaks to you and go for it. Surround yourself with like-minded people and soak up their knowledge.

A highly successful entrepreneur said, "Businesses don't fail; people give up."

Sometimes, giving up is the right decision. But usually, you just need to dig in and figure out how to make things better. What decisions are you making right now that are going to help you get to your landing-place? How do you clear that path to your destination? For me, getting ahead meant getting started. As long as I thought about writing a second book, nothing was happening. My achievement came when I connected it with action. You're going to make mistakes, but don't quit.

There are questions you have to ask yourself when you're ready to branch out and do your own thing. Are you a major risk-taker, medium or low risk? What character qualities do you want to look at within yourself to determine whether you can handle the risk, distress, the unknowns, the storms of being an entrepreneur? I transitioned before I took a big leap. You don't know when your dream will takeoff. There are just too many factors. Just know your best life is on the other side of your comfort zone.

I allowed myself time to grow into my comfort level and truly examined if this was God's move for me or simply personal desires. I wanted the freedom to work from home and enjoy the independence and flexibility of setting my schedule without reporting to anyone.

Be prepared to modify your plan if you need to, ready to react to any unforeseen surprises. Don't focus on thoughts of failure. It's just a part of life.

Sometimes it is the scariest unknowns that freeze our faith.

I wanted to live a bold Spirit-led life, so that meant bold focus. It also meant I had to stay prayed up. The enemy doesn't fight fair but uses our insecurities and fear of rejection against us. If the fear that creeps in doesn't derail our lives entirely, it keeps us so distracted that we fail to follow God's plan laid out for our lives.

And, when you're trying to live out your dream, you can't share it with everyone. Keep certain ideas and plans to yourself, or share them only with people who you know support your new season.

In life, you will realize there is a role for every person you meet. Different ones will test you, use you, love you and teach you. Those that are important are the ones who bring out the best in you, challenge you and accept you with all your faults. They are rare and amazing people.

Chapter 13

Praising God in the Face of Disappointment

Praise is powerful.

Praise can break an addiction.

Praise can turn a problem around.

Praise can break the chains of what holds you back.

You've probably heard the saying, "when the praises go up, the blessings come down."

But, that offers no comfort to people who have been praying and praising for months or years, and nothing changed. If you're going to pass the test, stop getting discouraged when circumstances tell you nothing is happening. Your doctor says you're not getting better, your financial situation is not changing, or your child has become someone you don't recognize. Every voice will tell you it's not going to work out.

In those moments, I try to drown out the discouraging voices plaguing my mind. I dig deep and fight with faith mixed with good ole fashioned grit.

In 1966, I remember being a part of what mom described as a late test experiment to integrate students. In the beginning, only ten percent of the top black students in my first-grade class were bussed to a nearby all-white school. A teacher was assigned to stay with me during recess at all times. Some of the black students were taunted and mistreated. I can still trace my middle-aged teacher's face in my mind—vanilla-colored skin, brown-haired, lightish eyes, nice teeth, and a sunny smile. She would lead me out back and hold my hand as we watched my classmates play together. They jumped about, their loud shrieks on the monkey bars and swings all signs of a half-hour of thrills and excitement. I can recall crying and being disappointed every day. I would seek comfort in my mom's arms because none of the new kids would play with me. Haunting thoughts ran rampant through my head that I was ostracized because I was black, that I wasn't good enough, that they feared me. Mom assured me things would get better and suggested I pray and ask God to help, so I did.

Three weeks later, she appeared at my feet—her strawberry blonde hair and missing front tooth with the widest grin.

She shouted, "Romona is your name, right? I'm Emily. You wanna play?"

Emily didn't seem bothered by the color of my skin. It took one small child to break the chains of my disappointment and integrate playtime. In the weeks and months that followed, I don't remember not having a playmate.

I learned even as a child some battles require you to continue praying and praising your way out even if you can't see a way out. Whenever I am in the battle, I try not to allow the anxiety and disappointments to drag me down. I believe faith is a training exercise.

You must stand strong and persevere through the pain. I know the saying, "God doesn't give us more than we can handle," but I believe at times, He does give us more than we can handle alone. Remember, God loves us, and through the journey, He is protecting and preparing us.

When you know it's God speaking an idea or plan into existence for your life, you can't let anything hold you back. Praise Him!

He wants you to change the way you think and act. He doesn't like hearing it's impossible to make changes in your life.

> *Thinking of possibilities is like driving a car on a freeway. You have an open road that stretches endlessly before you, where your thoughts are not shackled. But when we say, "impossible" we have already reached a dead-end in our minds. So dwell on possibilities to open your horizon.*
>
> —Pankaj Patel

A positive attitude will take you far when life disappoints.

Some of us are still trying to heal old, open wounds, believing that if we just ignore them, we will heal. Unfortunately, that hasn't worked in my life. There are times I had to flash my brights on my journey to let fear and disappointment know I'm still coming—no fog, wind or rain can get me off the path God charted for me. That's when you Praise Him!

You might be in a holding pattern right now. You're dissatisfied with your life. You haven't had a good break in months or years. You suffered a failed marriage, find it difficult to land a job or excel in your career and push toward your dreams. But there's a way you can put an end to the grounding of your life. You can get off the road to nowhere and soar to somewhere. That's when you Praise Him!

God didn't intend for us to be at war every day of our lives, wrestling with problems and fear.

He loves and understands us, and He wants us to thrive, not just survive. Why would we give our lives to Him if it meant misery and problems every day?

"For I know the plans I have for you," declares the Lord," plans to prosper you and not to harm you, plans to give you hope and a future." (Jeremiah 29:11, NIV)

When we truly start to have faith and stop fearing failure, believing in God's Word, our lives begin to change. Praise Him!

When trouble visits your doorstep, God will tell you if you should press on or if He has something else for you. Praise Him!

"Let us not become weary in doing good, for at the proper time we will reap a harvest if we do not give up." (Galatians: 6:9 NIV)

Some of you have been weary for a long time. You've been faithful. You've praised in pain, praised when it was unfair, praised when you were lonely, praised when everything around you seemed to be falling apart.

He will meet you where you are. When you're down and at your lowest, He will pick you up and prepare you for where He wants you to be.

The more you know God through His Word, the more clearly you can hear Him." Disappointments in your life won't last, but you have to get God involved. Praise the Lord!

What I've Learned... Gratitude

We live in such a fast-paced, on-demand world. We want our Uber on demand, our food and movies on demand, even our medicine. But we must still wait on God.

He cannot be rushed! His timing!

While you're waiting, there are miracles around us every day. Would we recognize one? We're in such a hurry. If we were just to slow down, be still and silent for a minute and be grateful for what we have.

When we focus on all the bad days, we miss out on all the good stuff. Stunning beauty surrounds us on earth. What if we ignored life's hiccups for a week? Put the computers, headphones and phones away for a couple of hours a day and cuddle more with our kids; take walks or jogs in the park; pray or meditate; grab a cup of coffee or drink with someone—just because. Close your eyes for a few minutes on the patio or porch, inhale and exhale, sniff the sights and sounds, and enjoy the stillness of nature. I love getting lost, when the Cleveland weather cooperates, becoming one with nature. I find God in the stillness, gratitude in the serenity, abundance in the silence. It forces you to mute the noise and enjoy the peace in your life.

Take the time to be thankful for your friends and family—being physically present with the people you care about.

We tend to be so focused on our schedule and busy lives. We think we're connecting with people by scrolling through our phone's Rolodex, texting, hitting them up in their DM's, but those are just empty calorie connections—quick, and they have no nourishment that can sustain a meaningful relationship.

I start my morning thanking God, not asking for what I don't have but being grateful for having enough, appreciating His blessings and favor in my life. I join hands with my husband, and we bow our heads in prayer when we wake, just praising God for his goodness and grace.

We praise Him, even if things are not going well, and ask for brighter days.

Thank Him for your children, your job, your car, your health, for your gifts and talents. Thank Him that you're grateful to be alive.

I believe abundant praise produces an abundant life. I know it's tough to believe when you're struggling, and you've been praying for months, and nothing changes. When that happened in my life, I started having a thankful heart, start thanking Him for His goodness, for His promises. I believe that gets His attention.

Having gratitude and being thankful even when you're in the midst of the storm is powerful.

One of my Romona's Kids, who I used to visit regularly at the Cleveland Clinic before she died, taught me a lot about gratitude and being thankful for each day.

"Blessed are the pure in heart, for they will see God." (Matthew 5:8 NIV)

Trina was a 7-year-old little brown-skinned beauty with a set of the most angelic big, brown eyes I had ever seen. Those deep-set beauties told a story—a story of innocence, yet grit. A story of pain, yet a fighter. She wore a bubbly smile that could light up Times Square and a heart as pure as gold. She possessed smiling eyes, yet a silent, almost untraceable fear. Trina knew without a lifesaving transplant, she would not survive, and amazingly, she shared with me that she was prepared to see God if He called.

She was born with a life-threatening form of Leukemia, a group of cancers of the blood that usually begin in the bone marrow and can result in a high number of abnormal blood cells. I met her after an interview I did with her and her grandmother, who was her caregiver. They wanted to increase awareness and hopefully encourage someone to donate the bone marrow she needed. The disease could be cruel on her tiny, nearly five-foot, 60-pound body. She was always fatigued, suffered bleeding and bruising, bouts of infection and more importantly to her, she wasn't like other kids who could run out and play, go to school and have a normal life. Until a bone marrow match could be found, every single Thursday she paid the hospital a visit to have several hours of blood transfusions. Every time I visited, she greeted me with the biggest smile.

I asked her one day how she was able to display such a cheerful spirit, even in the midst of her pain. She told a story of being thankful for her family, especially her frail grandmother, who was on the journey with her every single day. She was thankful for her doctors and nurses who lifted her spirit with toys and books and special treats. She expressed gratitude and the assurance that God would find a donor. I remember being stunned that a child so young could be filled with such insightful wisdom and faith.

One day I walked into her room and didn't greet her with my usual smile. I tried to force a crease in my lips. Trina sensed the tension in my body language and face and asked what was wrong.

"Miss Robinson, you know we greet one another with laughter, a smile and a hug. What's wrong?"

"Nothing's wrong girl. I'm just happy to see you sitting up and doing well," I said, flashing a big smile cheek to cheek.

I tried to hide the bad news her grandmother had just shared with me. Even though God delivered her miracle, and she found a donor, and the operation went well, the transplant was not a success.

"Actually, I'm not." She shocked me.

"What do you mean?"

"I feel awful, and even though the doctors haven't said, my body is showing signs that it may be rejecting the transplant."

My mind raced with thoughts of how to comfort her. Her perception was spot on—she needed no doctor to tell her she wasn't getting better. A tinge of guilt entered my heart because I was the adult, and I should have the words to bring her hope and faith. For her sake, I knew I needed mentally to snap out of my feelings of sadness and find a cheerful space in my head to boost and brighten her day.

She died four years later, but I will always remember the lessons learned from my pint-sized friend with a bold spiritual presence. She trusted God on good days and bad until the very end. She never focused on the illness that plagued her body. Instead, she cherished all of the other areas of her life she was thankful for.

This is an inextricable connection between joy and gratitude. I no longer take the simple things for granted, like my peace, my rest and play. I try to live each day like it's my last, unmoved by foolishness, instead, taking advantage of the greatest gift from God—my health and wellbeing, my friends, family and anyone I can help along the way.

Chapter 14

WHEN GOD SAYS, "YES!"

On a cool winter's night in 2019, I had a captive audience hanging on my every word. I was comfortable and in my element, giving a speech about my memoir in an Ohio theatre.

Suddenly, heat enveloped my head, my heart raced, beating at an abnormal pace. I paced back and forth on stage, trying to remember the last words I spoke. The stories in my book were becoming a blur. I felt extreme thirst, so I walked towards the podium, spotting bottled water left for me by event planners. I announced to the audience my intentions of quenching my thirst as I continued to walk and talk on my handheld wireless mic. I took a few gulps, and nothing changed. I slowly walked back to center stage, asking the audience, "Now where was I?" They laughed and shouted words they had last heard.

That was a great sign they were listening.

I glanced over at my husband in the front row, and I could see the look of concern on his face. He and I knew something no one else did. I had been sick for days. A salad for lunch two days before produced extreme vomiting. As a matter of fact, I don't ever recall being so sick. It produced a rush of heat and pain to my stomach, followed by a burst of nausea, and then I heaved. Seven times, I gagged and threw up. By midnight, when I felt my tortured body had no more food or water to excrete, we called the emergency room to see if he should bring me in. The nurse called the doctor on call, and he said just to sip water and other fluids to prevent nausea and dehydration. The next day, I felt better and was able to digest and hold down food and water, so I thought I was cured of the apparent food poisoning.

But there I was on stage and feeling like my body was depleted of any signs of normalcy. I tried, jokingly, to convince the audience that it might be better if I sat for a moment because of my heels, and I grabbed the only chair on stage and plopped down, not with my usual grace, which was another sign things were spinning out of control—and fast. I kept silently asking God to give me the strength to get through the speech. I was halfway there. But, the more energy I tried to exert, the worse it got. I had no choice. I was about to faint on stage, even in a sitting position.

I'm not sure what happened immediately afterward. I just recall a flurry of activity backstage behind the now drawn curtains to shield me from the audience's view. As paramedics laid me on a bench, I saw my husband, my girlfriend, Kelly, and the mayor.

EMT's were listening to my heart, checking my pulse, pricking my finger, wrapping my arm in a pad to take my blood pressure. Rodney told them about my marathon of vomiting two days prior. They started bombarding me with questions about how I felt, if I was dizzy, did I feel faint, my name, date of birth, was I able to walk.

One EMT shouted, "Her blood pressure is extremely high! Let's get her into the ambulance."

"That can't be," I shot back. "I've always had extremely good blood pressure. Are you sure I need to go to the hospital?"

The EMT answered calmly, but firmly. "Romona, you could have a blood clot or stroke with your heart working this hard to pump blood to it."

Once in the ambulance, they taped wires to my skin, inserted a needle with an IV, and checked my blood pressure and heart again.

In all the confusion, I had one calming constant, my husband. He never left my side. I watched this six foot, six inch, 245-pound man scrunch and cram his huge frame onto a five-foot couch a few feet away to stay with me overnight while emergency room doctors and nurses pumped five vials of water and electrolytes back into my body from extreme dehydration caused by the vomiting.

Unbeknownst to Rodney, I didn't sleep much that night. Instead, I watched him twist and turn, trying to find a comfortable position while he stood watch over me. I begged him to go home and return in the morning, but he would not hear of it, determined to make sure nothing happened to me.

At that moment, I knew this is what it feels like when God says yes.

I shared in *A Dirt Road to Somewhere* how I almost made the biggest mistake of my life by marrying Carl. My college sweetheart, and then-fiancé, left me hours after a laparoscopy, a surgery I needed to rule out cancer, when I was 26 years old.

Although minimally invasive, the procedure required placing a telescopic rod lens connected to a camera into my navel through a small incision. General anesthesia was required for the less than two-hour procedure. After the surgery, the doctor said I would be extremely sore. I would need help getting in and out of bed and bathing myself for a few days.

I was living in DC with the man I had planned to marry. We had practiced our vows "To have and to hold, in sickness and in health."

The doctor had great news. No cancer. It was a benign cyst. He sent me home with a clean bill of health. I was thankful it was not cancer, but I could barely walk. The laparoscopy left me in excruciating pain. I ambled like a zombie, even with Carl's help. Carl said he wanted to run a few errands after he got me home and tucked me in bed by 5:00 p.m. A few hours turned into a marathon of waiting. My fiancé, the man I was about to pledge my life to under God, returned at 5:30 a.m.

I had laid in a wet bed for hours. I couldn't take it anymore. As I moved toward the edge of the bed to clean myself up, I misjudged the distance and fell onto the floor, busting my stitches. Rubbing my fingers over the wound, I felt blood escaping my body.

That night on the floor, an alarm went off in my head. This was not the type of man God chose for me—a man who abandoned me when I needed him the most.

Now, during one of the most frightening nights of my life, my godsend—my husband. The man I prayed for, waited for, and trusted God to do His work in His timing.

My thoughts drifted back to 2003 at the infamous Watergate Hotel in Washington, DC. Rodney and I had been dating for eight months, enduring a commuter relationship, traveling between Cleveland and DC for dates. That night we were enjoying a beautiful candlelit dinner, and I had no idea a proposal was coming. How could I? We often went to exceptional restaurants when I visited DC. I did notice he seemed uncharacteristically nervous. Even our waiter was a bit anxious.

I tried to be engaging, talking about the history of the Watergate, and Rodney was mostly nodding his head, looking disinterested in the conversation. I chalked it up to the fact that the entire restaurant was abuzz with gossip because former Secretary of State, Condoleezza Rice, arrived with a full entourage of Secret Service members shortly after we were seated. She sat three tables away from us, and security was inconspicuous, yet visible.

For the first time in our short dating span, Rodney was speechless. I questioned if he was okay. Since he held a job as a contractor at the State Department, I wondered if her presence bothered him, or the Secret Service that kept staring at us. I would slowly lift my fork, trying not to make any sudden gestures, fearing they might come to tackle me. That's truly how I felt with their peering eyes. The reason for his nervous energy would soon reveal itself.

Our waiter poured champagne, and Rodney toasted our courtship and professed his love for me. He slid back his chair, stood up and got down on bended knee, and asked me for my hand in marriage. The Secret Service watched his every move. He couldn't have choreographed it any better. I said yes, to the applause of onlookers. We were married a year later.

Now, here we were nearly fifteen years later facing our first health scare, and he stayed by my side.

God finally saying yes meant I had a true partner who lived by the vows he took. The man determined to nurse me back to health after I was diagnosed with severe dehydration brought on by a stomach virus. I finally had someone who would take care of me when I couldn't.

I lay there thinking about my blessed marriage, how we had grown from newlyweds fighting to get our way and to be heard, to seasoned partners who know marriage isn't 50/50. At times, one of us gets the short end of the stick, but we're okay with that. It works for us. I reminisced about the tough times. How after my third and fourth miscarriage, no words were spoken. He would simply lay behind me and rock me to sleep at night, praying for my mental and physical healing. The time when I screamed in agony on a cruise ship vacation after getting my hand caught in a two-ton steel door, he ran to my rescue, and of all things, it was the diamond on my wedding ring he bought me that prevented me from losing my fingers. He picked me up off the floor when I couldn't rise under my own strength after my beloved mom passed suddenly, and my whole world seemed to spin out of control in an instant.

Our marriage is one of the places in the world where we feel the strongest and safest. We have found a balance of respect allowing each other to be heard. Our love, commitment, trust and good communication is paramount. But so is patience, forgiveness and selflessness.

And, wow God, you threw in a lot of laughter and humor. My husband can be one of the funniest people in the room. But when it comes to our Lord and Savior, he is a praying man who believes more fiercely than anyone I know that God is the answer and the way.

"For husbands, this means love your wives, just as Christ loved the church. He gave up his life for her." (Ephesians 5:25 NIV)

Scripture says husbands should love their wives exactly like Christ did—a love marked by giving, not getting. We don't like waiting on anything—not at the doctor's office, at the DMV, not for our fast food or coffee. We are an impatient society.

But, God cannot be rushed.

"But as for me, I watch in the hope for the LORD, I will wait for God my Savior; my God will hear me." (Micah 7:7 NIV)

Like many of you, earlier in my life, I grew tired of waiting on God. Everyone around me seemed to have someone, so I became disobedient, trying to get ahead of Him and kept dating men who were all wrong for me. God put up the roadblocks, but I went around them. I'll admit it, sometimes they were just super fine, and I was extremely lonely or just wanted companionship. But that's not how waiting on God works. I believe he doesn't want us sacrificing our beliefs, our integrity, morals, and value as a woman.

"Be happy in your hope. Do not give up when trouble comes. Do not let anything stop you from praying." (Romans 12:12 NLT)

In the Message Bible, the same verse reads, "Don't burn out; keep yourselves fueled and aflame. Be alert servants of the Master, cheerfully expectant. Don't quit in hard times; pray all the harder."

That was the key to for me when God finally said yes. I had started praying harder. I had stopped trying to go it alone and got God involved. I didn't sit around, feeling sad. Instead, I went out into the world and enjoyed life, knowing when God had tinkered with me enough, grown my faith, and got me ready He would send a mate.

"The Lord God said, 'It is not good for the man to be alone. I will make a helper suitable for him.'" (Genesis 2:18 NIV)

If you want a suitable partner, know that God sees you and hears you. He just might be trying to do some work in you first. One of my friends says she's waiting on God in one breath to send her a mate, but in another, she'll confide she's set in her ways and doesn't know at her age if she'd be willing to compromise in a relationship. I told her God already knows about her strengths and weaknesses, her wants and needs, even better than she does. He knows you too.

God had to grow patience in me. I've always been unbelievably impatient, a stickler for time. I would get heated if people were fifteen minutes late without calling and hated procrastinators. I had to learn we're all different, and there are things about me that were not perfect, and that was okay. But, if you're not ready to compromise, you're not ready for marriage. My wonderful husband, with his huge up side, is a procrastinator! And I would choose him a thousand times more. I think that is God's sense of humor.

What I've Learned...
What's on your Wait List?

So what's on your wait list? Maybe it's not a mate. A new job or promotion? Waiting for your health to improve, you want a new home? Are you plagued by financial worries, concerned about the path your kids are on? No matter what you've been praying and asking God for, the wait can be excruciating, especially when there is no evidence he is listening.

Even when I sank to my lowest battling obstacles and issues waiting for God to answer my prayers, it was my faith I needed to continue to grow.

I've found that sometimes the Lord is waiting for growth in us. It's up to you to decide what that means. Making changes in your life requires heart work and head work. It can be hard to change when you've always done it one way.

It's also human nature to have self-doubt and insecurities, from time-to-time, that God doesn't care about you. It becomes a problem when it controls your choices, when it feeds on your heart, and you become someone you're not—alone and desperate because you tire of waiting for God to grant the things you've been praying about.

An acquaintance asked me to talk to her rebellious teenager. She was so worried she was going to ruin her life and become promiscuous. I asked her daughter why she had started to wear skirts up her rear, why she felt she needed to make a drastic change in her wardrobe. She told me it was because of her low self-esteem and lack of confidence. She wanted to date like her friends, but none of the boys were attracted to her.

I responded, "I would not have guessed you lacked confidence the way to strut around in those tight, very short skirts and shorts, and you're always the loudest person in the room."

She confided. It was all an act. She felt she needed to play the role of a loud-mouthed, in-your-face girl to get attention and compete with girls who were prettier and sported a heavy dose of self-esteem. Raised in the church, she prayed, asking God for a young beau to like her.

When you try to get someone to see the beauty they possess that is uniquely created by God, it can fall on deaf ears, especially with teens. They live in the now, bombarded with social media and the pressure to fit in and live up to the hype. Recent studies show anxiety levels among teens are at an all-time high. Every time I would see this girl, she was never alone and always surrounded by other youngsters—she seemed to be a friend magnet.

I pressed her on why she thought people enjoyed her company. "Do you think it is your clothing?"

"Kids love my fun personality. I'm outgoing and one of the dope kids."

"So you don't need the risqué clothing to attract friends, do you? And if you want to attract boys, trust me, it's the wrong kind of young man," I said sternly. What do you see when you look in the mirror?"

"I don't see any outward beauty, but I have a pretty smile."

"I see so much more in you," I told her. "You're smart as a whip, quick-witted, and I laugh every time we talk. No wonder people want to be around you. We enjoy conversations about politics! Do you know how many teens can have a fluent conversation with me about policy in Washington, Kim Jong-un and the Russia elections meddling?" I laughed. "Those smart, intuitive and worldly qualities you possess are gifts from God. They are natural gifts that belong to you, and they are all you need to attract the right kind of friends. The new clothing will get you a lot of stares, but it will not build your confidence, and it will definitely not get you a suitable mate."

She agreed to lower her hot pants by an inch or two. (Hey, Rome wasn't built in a day!)

While you're waiting on God to say yes, He's waiting for you to face your fears of rejection and work on why you do the things you do—it is truly liberating. It becomes easier to reject the brainwashing by Satan to make you feel like you're not pretty enough, people don't like you, you're odd, an outcast or worthless.

The control freak in us wants to rush things along and change the situation ourselves. We go ahead and around God, pushing past the barriers He put in place, trying to find answers and direction immediately.

But waiting on God means you're trusting His Word. "Delight yourself in the Lord, and he will give you the desires of your heart. Commit your way to the Lord; trust in him, and he will act." (Psalm 37:4-5 ESV)

He knows when you've done the work on you, and you're ready for a yes!

Chapter 15

God Promises an Abundant Life

I finally forced myself to actually open Mom's Bible she was reading before she died. It was a new one I bought her three months before she passed. She would rave about how much she loved the leather-bound feel of it and especially the large text. My sister said she was reading scripture at a feverish pitch in the days before her death. Throughout my childhood, Mom always marked her Bible with a pen and bits and scraps of paper, and she'd outline verses that touched her senses.

When I first reached for the brown and burgundy bible, I spotted a piece of a torn paper towel peeking out from one of its pages. My sister said Mom had been reading the book of John right before the last seizure that took her life. My heart pounded, and I took deep breathes as I attempted to open the pages to see what was on her mind before the Lord brought her home. For days, I couldn't do it. The book remained closed.

On a wintry February night, I snuggled on my comfy brown sofa with a throw to warm my legs and slid her Bible off the coffee table. I handled it delicately as if it were a newborn baby being gently and carefully delivered to its mom for the first time. I stroked it, caressed it, taking it into my arms, and thrusting it against my heart—hoping I could feel or smell some semblance of her. My mind and elevated heartbeat raced with thoughts of sadness and happiness, joy and pain, love and loss. My emotions danced back and forth, giving me the green light to choose what mental space I wanted to be in before I started to read. I was careful not to disturb its contents. In addition to the paper towel, I could see what looked like a business card placed between one of the pages.

My eyes fixated on the paper towel since I knew that's what Mom used as a bookmarker to remember where she left off reading scripture, knowing it was likely the last scripture she read the night before she was admitted to the hospital and later died. I was transplanted back to that awful day she passed and remembering the sounds of doctors working feverishly to save her. My faith in God's healing power drew me back to her paper towel. I was ready to see what she was reading.

"For God so loved the world that he gave his one and only Son, that whoever believes in him shall not perish but have eternal life." (John 3:16 NIV)

I was shocked that she was reading not just the book of John but that particular passage. Mom had given her life to the Lord as a little girl. But was she questioning where she was going? Did she need assurances from the Word, or was the scripture just comforting during a time she apparently knew was drawing near?

As I flipped and gently caressed the pages, knowing her hands had been there, I stopped at John 10:10. She had an asterisk beside the verse.

"The thief does not come except to steal, and to kill, and to destroy. I have come that they may have life, and that they may have it more abundantly."

I smiled, thankful Mom knew, despite the dementia, which was robbing her of her mind and memory. She weathered the storms always with the assurance we would have enough.

My face filled with joy, remembering how we all received this abundant life the moment we accepted Him as our Savior. I am grateful she experienced abundance later in life when her children helped to provide her with earthly comforts like her home and car and never a worry about going without. But it was her God who provided the abundance spiritually and mentally.

I was comforted by knowing in her last days she was talking about all the blessings God granted her. She talked about fishing with her dad, who had been gone since she was 12. She called out all of her eleven children by name, and that's hard for me to do without pause.

My mind drifted back to a more pleasant time. I could hear the wind rustling through the cornfields that flanked my childhood home, producing a whiff of animal manure from 30 or so farm animals in our chicken coop. The aroma would be disgusting to most, but for me, it produced sweet memories of my time in the garden with Mom.

She gained such joy in sowing her seeds. In a town where everyone struggled, you bartered a lot. Mom would share an abundant harvest from the garden with a few of the senior ladies on tight fixed incomes who might need a little extra food.

I can still sketch a portrait of the people who knocked on our door, hoping Mom's harvest had produced enough to share. Some would offer to pay her, but Mom never took money for what she called God's blessing. We were schooled to do the same. If you have more than enough, put some back for a raining day, and share the rest with those less fortunate.

Mom would always invite her friends, Miss Johnson and Miss Tucker, over after an overflow of goodness from the garden. They would cozy up to the kitchen table sipping coffee, eating graham crackers, and commodity cheese, or whatever Mom could scrounge up to serve. I watched the trio talk about the latest gossip in our tiny town and share dark stories about their harsh reality of barely getting by. Mostly though, they talked about why they were visiting, Mom's garden.

I can recall many memories of Ms. Tucker or Ms. Johnson yelling out like Mom was in the next room and not right there in front of them.

"Henrutta, it's how they pronounced Henrietta, you got any extra collards or turnips you can spare?"

"I got a few extra bags of government beans and cheese I can share with yo chireens, if you need it," they would offer.

"I sho do," Mom responded, thrilled she could help her senior neighbors. "Romona, grab an armful of those plastic grocery bags we stoh (store) under the kitchen sank so we can stuff some turn-ups and stuff in 'em."

"My, my, Henrutta, you sho (sure) do grow a nice crop of greens. How in the world do you get'em to turn out like this?"

"Chile, you got that magic touch," they would say.

"No, it's mo (more) like God's touch. I do pretty good when we have pretty good rains and normal temperatures during the plantin' season. The Lawd has blessed me with plenty to share," Mom would explain.

"Are you sho you not using somethin' special you keepin' from us?"

"Nah, I jus' plant my seeds the way my daddy used to. I work hard out there. When I can afford to buy good topsoil, I produce an even better harvest. Most times, I mix it with the manure outback or that boy who lives up the street will brang me a truckload of fertiliza'," Momma shared.

I'm not sure what that stuff was mixed with. It's some of the foulest/stankiest smelling mixture, but it works!

I used to wonder how something so foul (it stank to high heaven is the phrase we used to use) could produce some of the freshest and tastiest deliciousness on earth.

That kind of joy Mom got from giving to others probably produced the yearning in me to serve others as well.

She taught me a lot about sharing and giving to those less fortunate. I learned by example when she had us pick oversized bowls of tomatoes, collards, turn-up, okra and snap peas and store them just in case someone else came by in need.

I'm so thankful I was brave enough to finally open Mom's Bible and allow the scriptures she was reading to stir up such wonderful memories about the true meaning of blessings from God.

Mom's garden taught me so many lessons on abundance.

Growing up in poverty in Wilson City, I never knew I would someday see the beauty in it. A little girl being put to work in the soybean fields at 10 years old—a child who worked and struggled so hard to help my mom make ends meet—now filled with gratitude for a God-driven life. The sweat and tears of working so hard—yet still having so little—used to draw thoughts of shame—feelings that I did not and would not ever measure up to the other kids.

But a supernatural peace comes from walking with God and watching Him work in your life. It's sort of an out-of-body experience. I can only describe it one way.

I found peace and serenity in memories of being with Mom in the garden like no other place on earth. It's was a place where you could find yourself and lose yourself in your thoughts. A place to question your passion for the art of gardening when the crops didn't cooperate. A place to explore, cultivate the courage to chart a new path in life. A time to explore your failures and successes. A field of solitude. A space to express your joy and frustrations. The spot where there are sometimes unspoken words. Just you being one with nature—surrounded by God's creations.

I started to think back to Moms life. At first glance, all you could see was a woman who struggled all of her life to provide a better future for her kids—one she prayed would not include poverty like generations past. But, when you looked closely, you saw a life well lived—a satisfied soul filled with abundance.

Yes, she raised her children in poverty, but she shared the riches God had given her with others—not monetary, but wisdom, the kind you can't buy—God-filled. The care and success of her children was her pride and joy. She was extremely proud of her two years in college, although she always wished she could have finished. Mom, you deserve an honorary degree for all you endured.

There were times Mom wore masks, usually from her kids, sheltering us from the extreme pressures of trying to feed and clothe us. But what she didn't hide was the ability to deal with whatever life threw her way.

Mom didn't settle for status quo. She never wallowed in self-pity proclaiming, "I've had bad breaks, deserted by men, so this is all there is for us." She never said, "I'm just going to sit in this poverty that has plagued the generations before me."

Mom knew she was not limited by where she came from, her parents, her neighborhood, and she didn't let circumstances discourage her.

I am so full. I'm grateful for my faith-filled life. I'm thankful for the opportunity to share my journey down some well-lit and pitch-black roads. No matter my travels, smooth or bumpy, my undying faith tells me God is there providing that guiding light when I need it. Eliminating fear and allowing faith, room to grow doesn't happen overnight. It takes time.

I want you to believe you don't have to settle where you are.

It doesn't have to be the end of the road because of past mistakes—you can turn around. If it dead-ends—try something different.

My journey has been part spiritual awakening and part embracing the beautiful course God laid out for me. The beauty is in not knowing where my destination will lead me.

I am a product of a woman who never asked for a handout, even when she probably should have. She never allowed barricades and barriers to block her path and that of her children. I can still hear the rally cry she must have screamed a thousand times growing up.

"I'm raisin' you down here on this dead-end dirt road that goes to nowhere, but you are goin' somewhere!"

She was right. I did go somewhere. Now that she is gone, she has left me with my own brand of insight and wisdom through a battle-tested life—one I can now share with others.

More than anything, living an abundant life is about living a full life, allowing God the space to work. If you can, wake up in the morning and think, "No matter what gets done and how much I have left undone, I will not give up." Don't take negative thoughts to bed with you—thinking I am imperfect, inadequate, afraid, and I have no one. Instead, try winding down with thoughts of gratitude that you are enough in God's eyes, and tomorrow is a new chance for new connections.

Some people have everything, but they still feel poor. Others have less, but they feel abundant. It's all the result of your perspective. If you are grateful to God, He'll fill your life with more to be grateful for.

As I continued to pour over Mom's Bible, I was curious about the business card she had placed between the pages.

It was a card about hospice care. My heart cringed and sunk. I leaned over in a ball of hurt. I had no idea anyone had talked to my mom about hospice. She was not that ill, I thought. Could she have been talking to someone without our knowledge? I wondered. The card was placed next to Genesis chapter 1 toward the end.

Then God said, "I give you every seed-bearing plant on the face of the whole earth and every tree that has fruit with seed in it. They will be yours for food." (Genesis 1:29, NIV)

I started to wonder about my mom's last weeks on earth. Why she was interested in Genesis, the beginning. Was she thanking Him for the seeds she planted that produced plentiful fruit for her and her children? I will never know this side of heaven, but I felt a closeness to her, and my spirit felt a connection to the scripture I know provided her peace and comfort in her last days.

I found peace in knowing you don't have to try and figure out everything. Some things just are. The Word of God will keep you on track.

God has used my journey to touch more lives than I ever could have imagined. Why would I question His plan? He already knows how my journey ends, and I'm excited to see where this ride takes me next. I am completely comfortable with Him in the driver's seat.

EPILOGUE

Your Best Life

If I'm not living my best life, I'm pretty darn near it. I finally feel totally good in my own skin. I am now at the age when every day is precious. I have lived more years than I have left on this earth, and I plan to continue to live life to the fullest. I love showing acts of kindness every day. I try to do something or say something that puts a smile on someone else's face. It is a small commitment, one that I enjoy. I love waking up in the morning, praying, then meditating, then posting a Thought of the Day on my social media pages in hopes of brightening someone else's morning. I enjoy being present in the lives of people who matter to me and strangers who might need a kind word.

I have a renewed sense of who I am, and fear doesn't rock me much anymore. Maybe it has something to do with maturity. For me, it has been aging in grace, life seems sufficient. You don't complain as much, and you definitely are not moved by nonsense. Triggers that used to push you to fly off the handle are just dusted off your shoulders like swatting a pesky mosquito. It can only bite you if it lands and sticks, and you're done with bloodsuckers, so no worries.

"Like newborn babies, crave pure spiritual milk, so that by it you may grow up in your salvation, now that you have tasted that the Lord is good." (1 Peter 2:2-3 NIV)

Reading the scripture isn't enough. God has the power, but you have to help yourself by taking action and cleaning house. Get rid of malice in your life. Do a clean sweep of envy and hurtful talk that can enter your space. Wipe away the pretense. You don't have to meticulously edit yourself, cutting out the weak parts you don't like, sharing with the world only your strengths. It's okay if you're flawed. We all are. We even have built-in filters that prevent us from speaking what we're actually feeling and thinking. But, when you deny your own voice, you are hiding the authentic you. You are giving up your power.

You don't have to fear going it alone. He will be right there with you—but you have to truly believe His Word. No more waiting for the "perfect time." No more playing it small and staying stuck. Stop letting worry overwhelm you. You are old enough to wake up to your calling and live your dream. It is never too early or too late.

I hope this book inspires you to act. Dig deep and look inside yourself. Tell yourself you have what it takes to make your life better. There is no fake it 'til you make it when it comes to what you want—what God's designed for you. Go out and get it.

I have chosen to live a life of integrity and grace. I refused to settle for less than what I know God intended for me, whether in a relationship or in my career. Speaking your truth and asking for what you want might be off-putting to some. It may even create conflict or tension, but I've learned to take charge of my life and live in peace and harmony, not allowing others to steal my joy. Stop telling yourself you aren't strong enough, you are! *Your voice can manipulate and persuade you to make the wrong choices. Why not use it as God intended, a verbal instrument to teach, motivate, inspire, to do good works.*

"The soothing tongue is a tree of life, but a perverse tongue crushes the spirit." (Proverbs 15:4 NIV)

Kind words heal and help, cutting words wound and maim as this scripture says in the Message Bible. The day I started living by the Word and stopped excepting mediocrity, messiness and negativity, my vision of how I wanted to live my best life became clearer.

Do you know what your best life looks like for you? Don't be shy about what you want your future to look like, speak up, speak out and claim it.

God says, "You have not because you ask not." (James 4:2)

When you learn to put others before yourselves, you will start to see blessings in your life. God loves a cheerful giver, especially those who take care of his flock who are less fortunate. Selflessness is key, and giving more of yourself is expected.

Someone told me recently, "Romona, it's okay to put yourself first. It doesn't mean you're selfish or unkind."

Those words created a kind of panic in my head and heart. But why? It is true. I talked about it earlier. You can't help others if you don't first take care of you. God will create a balance when you seek His way.

When you surround yourself with blessed people you will start to look like who you are connected to. If you follow evildoers and people who are going nowhere, that evil will devour you.

In this life, don't be afraid to rock the boat. I never liked the saying, Stay in your Lane. Says who? Some felt that way when I entered the male-dominated broadcast industry.

Had I "stayed in my lane" in the '80s and not pushed past the roadblocks to find my somewhere, I might not have become a journalist. Step out of your comfort zone and cross any lane on your journey you darn well please.

> *Be fearless. Have the courage to take risks. Go where there are no guarantees. Get out of your comfort zone even if it means being uncomfortable.*
>
> *The road less traveled is sometimes fraught with barricades, bumps and unchartered terrain. But it is on that road where your character is truly tested and have the courage to accept that you're not perfect, nothing is and no one is—and that's OK.*
>
> —Katie Couric

I love that quote from one of my news faves.

In my new walk, I'm allowing God to grow me and use me to speak to readers about everything I've learned on the road God mapped out for me.

I recently called to make a dinner reservation, and the young lady on the other end said, "Miss Robinson, you have such a nice voice. I have listened and followed you as a child. It's such a powerful voice," she went on to say.

I know she meant my oratorical tone, but she reminded me God had given me a voice to spread more love and kindness in the universe. We all have that capability—to speak up, to use our voice to demand a better future for ourselves and our children.

I started to live a good life when I stopped worrying about what everybody thinks. If you change with every criticism, you're going to live a life of confusion trying to live up to someone else's expectations, trying to win their favor. It's God favor that you should seek. I spent a long time trying not to disappoint people.

I gave away a lot of money because I wanted to be liked. Once I learned that no is not a bad word, and it is okay to disappoint some people, I started living my best life.

People fit you into their box, and when they see you as a box of stupid, they will keep you stored and open the box whenever they need to use you. I know it sounds harsh, but it's true. I allowed myself to be mistreated.

Some of us sabotage our own lives. In striving for success, I was so focused on my destination I forgot to enjoy the incredible experiences that got me here. But I do today. The saying is true, "There are two important days of our lives: The day we are born, and the day we realize why we were born." I discovered my purpose when I listened to God's voice.

He has done some emotional tinkering upstairs, and I was no longer afraid to go out into the world—places known and unknown to share my testimony. I started posting my love for Christ on my social media pages. I no longer cared if people thought I was a religious quack. I started to spread the word about His goodness and grace if you accept Him. My husband and I started weekly spiritual testimonies on Facebook and Instagram, a short video on how God can help solve everyday problems in your life if you believe in Him and trust Him.

Living my best life is still a work in progress and moving forward, rarely looking back at past mistakes. Sometimes, it took sadness to help me recognize real happiness. I needed to experience loneliness to value good company. I had to allow the outside noise to appreciate silence. I had to be challenged to find the power in my voice. Enduring heartache and pain strengthened me.

Most of all, I needed to go up against fear to grow my faith.

Acknowledgements

It takes a village to publish a book, and I thank God for the incredible people he surrounded me with.

My developmental editor, Melissa Wuske, who first tackled my raw manuscript. You're a brave woman. Thank you for bringing focus and clarity to my work. My book editor Lisa Bell, what a talent. Your skilled editing helped provide the flow, cohesiveness and fine-tuning my manuscript lacked. Your advice was invaluable.

Lisa Umina and the Halo Publishing International team: I am thrilled to become a series author in your professional hands. You and your team once again exceeded expectations, providing expert guidance and a wonderful publishing experience.

Judge Brown and Amy Lechko, words cannot express my gratitude for your praises about the book.

To my friend Kelly Banks, you should be paid for your wise counsel. You have a way of combining book and common sense that makes my approach to writing clearer.

I turned to friend Kim Anderson for real talk. Your feedback was always honest and direct just the way I like it.

Melanie Kennedy, my kindred spirit. How does a young soul have so much wisdom? Your suggestions were on point.

My sister-in-law Ramona Tyler, your eagerness to read my manuscript and provide feedback fueled my writing and creativity.

Words cannot express my appreciation for my dear sister, Melissa, who endured countless phone calls and emails about the book. You are truly a Godsend. I bombarded you with a litany of changes, and you read them all and offered critical advice. Nephew Sebastion and sister Rena, thank you for offering immeasurable suggestions about going deeper in my transparency for younger readers who might be starved for wisdom.

My loving husband Rodney, who would wake up in the wee hours of the morning when I had a new idea for the book, and I had to write it down. You never complained. I love you for accepting my writing energy bursts even when they came at the most inopportune time.

To the many friends and strangers who provided helpful advice and offered to help, I thank you for your support and kindness.

About Romona

Romona Robinson is an eight-time Emmy Award-winning journalist, with 30 years of public speaking experience. She is a national award-winning author of *A Dirt Road to Somewhere* and now *Your Voice is Your Power*.

She is founder of Romona's Kids, an Emmy nominated television program-turned-institution in Cleveland she started in 1990 to empower and encourage youth to find their path.

Romona is a television trailblazer becoming the first black female to anchor an evening broadcast in Cleveland. She was also the first woman to solo anchor an evening newscast in the city. She is one of the most well-respected and admired journalists in Northeast Ohio, having earned the trust of viewers for her integrity and unbiased reporting.

As a journalist, Romona has traveled the country, covering presidents and world leaders, including Nelson Mandela and the late Ronald Reagan. In 2011, she garnered a rare, exclusive interview with President Barack Obama.

Along with her colleagues at station WOIO-TV 19, where she served as primary anchor, Romona won the coveted Edward R. Murrow Award in 2014. She was inducted into the Press Club of Cleveland's Journalism Hall of Fame in 2016 and had the honor of receiving EWAW's Alpha Woman Award in 2017, which is given to women who exemplify strength in their field and use it to empower other women.

For 20 years, Romona served as the honorary chair of the Komen Race for the Cure, helping to bring awareness and hope to countless women. Romona's tireless work with children and her dedication to diversity issues have earned her such prestigious awards as the YWCA's Women of Achievement Award and The Diversity in Media Award.

Romona is also recognized for her powerful, dynamic messages as a motivational speaker.

Romona earned a Bachelor of Science degree in broadcast journalism from Lincoln University in Jefferson City, Missouri. Now, Romona is frequently called upon to speak to women and children who need empowering messages of faith, hope, determination, and perseverance. She has blanketed the state of Ohio and other parts of the nation, attending events from corporate affairs to meetings of various women's organizations. She firmly believes we all have something to offer to the world—we just have to allow God to lead us.

Stay Connected with Romona

Online:
romonarobinson.com

Instagram:
@RomonaRobinson

Facebook:
@RomonaRobinson19
@Romona Robinson

Twitter:
@romonarobinson

LinkedIn:
Romona Robinson

If you enjoyed my book, an Amazon review would be greatly appreciated.

Part of the proceeds of this book will be donated to organizations that serve the needs of children.

Contact Romona Robinson:

Website: romonarobinson.com

Telephone: 800-296-8232

CPSIA information can be obtained
at www.ICGtesting.com
Printed in the USA
BVHW041037120919
558226BV00005B/13/P

9 781612 447698